RSPB

GREAT BRITISH

BIRDWATCHER'S

PUZZLE BOOK

GREAT BRITISH
BIRDWATCHER'S
PUZZLE BOOK

DOMINIC COUZENS
WITH
DR GARETH MOORE

First published in Great Britain in 2022 by Gaia, an imprint of
Octopus Publishing Group Ltd
Carmelite House
50 Victoria Embankment
London EC4Y 0DZ

In association with the RSPB.

www.octopusbooks.co.uk

An Hachette UK Company
www.hachette.co.uk

Text copyright © Dominic Couzens 2022
Puzzles copyright © Any Puzzle Media Ltd 2022
Design copyright © Octopus Publishing Group 2022

Distributed in the US by
Hachette Book Group
1290 Avenue of the Americas
4th and 5th Floors
New York, NY 10104

Distributed in Canada by
Canadian Manda Group
664 Annette St.
Toronto, Ontario, Canada M6S 2C8

Edited and designed by Design23.

ISBN 978-1-85675-496-5

A CIP catalogue record for this book is available from the British Library.

Printed and bound in Great Britain

10 9 8 7 6 5 4

This FSC® label means that materials used for the product have been responsibly sourced

Commissioning Editor: Nicola Crane
Creative Director: Jonathan Christie
Designer: Design23
Editor: Sarah Kyle
Deputy Picture Manager: Jennifer Veall
Production Manager: Lisa Pinnell

Manufactured under licence from RSPB Sales Limited to raise awareness of the RSPB (charity registration in England and Wales no 207076 and Scotland no SC037654).

For all licensed Products sold by Octopus Publishing Group Limited, Octopus Publishing Group Limited will donate a minimum of £4,000 through an Advance and Royalty payments to RSPB Sales Ltd, which gives all its distributable profits through Gift Aid to the RSPB.

Contents

ABOUT THE AUTHORS

Dominic Couzens is a leading nature writer and lecturer in the UK. He has been writing about wildlife for over 30 years and is the author of many successful books including *Secret Lives of Garden Birds*, *A Bird a Day* and *ID Guide to Garden Insects of Britain and NW Europe*. Dominic has appeared on BBC television and regularly contributes to leading magazines including *BBC Wildlife* Magazine, *Birdwatching*, *BBC Countryfile* and the *Guardian* Country Diary. He currently lives in Dorset.

Dr Gareth Moore has authored numerous bestselling puzzle books, including *The Ordnance Survey Puzzle Book* and *The Mindfulness Puzzle Book*. Dubbed 'Britain's King of Puzzles' by the *Sun*, his books have sold in excess of 5 million copies in English alone, and have been translated into over 35 languages.

ABOUT THE RSPB

The RSPB is the UK's largest nature conservation charity. We work locally in the UK, and around the world.

Our vision is a shared world where wildlife, wild places and all people thrive. We protect and restore habitats, save species, share our knowledge and connect people with nature.

Protecting nature is a huge task, so we work together with other organisations, governments, businesses and individuals to build a world where nature thrives.

Led by science, our work ranges from everyday actions that help protect and restore natural environments and save species to global conservation that you can see from space.

Our supporters are helping us to end the nature and climate emergency. Please do what you can to support our wildlife.

Nature is in crisis. Together we can save it.

By purchasing this book you are helping to fund the RSPB's conservation work.

Visit **rspb.org.uk** for more information.

INTRODUCTION

This quiz book is a test of your all-round knowledge of British birds. It is designed to satisfy all levels of ability. Some of the quizzes are easy – even silly – and some are very difficult, with many levels in between. Hopefully there is fun for everyone within these pages. Even if the only bird you know is a robin, don't despair – there is a whole quiz on those (see page 29).

The first question to ask, of course, is what is a British bird? Strictly speaking, it is any species on the British List, which is maintained by the British Ornithologists' Union (bou.org.uk/british-list). Remarkably, to date more than 600 species have been recorded in the wild since 1800, many of them being very rare. For this quiz book, however, I have instead used the birds selected for the *RSPB Handbook of British Birds*, Fifth Edition (Holden and Gregory 2021), which has about 300 species, and generally only the better known of these. There is one section called 'A Rare Sight', which does include all the extra rarities, and will hopefully titillate the more experienced birders among us.

The quizzes will test you on such subjects as bird names, birds in culture, bird biology, bird behaviour, migration and so on. Two of the sections are collections of questions about particular birds: first, garden birds and secondly, birds of coast and country, the sorts of species you might see on a day trip away from home, or on holiday.

All the quiz formats will be familiar. There are straight general knowledge questions, multiple choice answers, mix-and-match compilations, true or false selections, 'What Bird Am I?' clues, crosswords, wordsearches and much more. In the middle of the book, you will find a series of illustrations for you to identify. There are migration route maps and missing words. There is even a series of fascinating facts dotted about, which don't actually ask questions. Everyone will find their favourites.

Everyone will also find the answers. These are referenced at the bottom of each page. Basically, there is one point for each correct answer, unless otherwise specified. There is half a mark if you're almost right – and how 'almost' is entirely up to you.

There is always a danger in taking any book too seriously, let alone a quiz book like this, but with more than 1,000 questions, it is a mine of information. It is my fond hope that, besides being fun, this book will also shine a small light on the incredible world of birds and amaze you as much as it tests you. Of course, certain species are more common in some areas than in others, so we all see different birds on a daily basis. With that in mind, the questions should help people everywhere to appreciate birds far more, and wish to preserve them a little more, too.

Dominic Couzens

CHAPTER ONE

GREAT GARDEN BIRDS

Hidden Names

Can you find the names of some familiar birds hidden in these sentences?

1. The siblings used to spar, row and argue all the time.

2. The sergeant said that his platoon had a pretty meagre attitude to hard work.

3. The homemade brew rendered them virtually incapacitated!

4. I am still smarting from the comments you made!

5. I didn't expect to see all those hippos wallowing in the mud.

6. I personally found the movie Men In Black captivating.

7. There is no doubt that members of the club lack birding experience.

8. It's nice to see the pole star lingering in the sky.

9. She is a good organiser, and that's her one good point, I think.

10. I'm not a great fan of your crooked nose, to be honest.

Pathfinder

Can you find six types of tit in the grid below, as well as one very small interloper which is occasionally seen flocking with tits? Starting at the shaded square, find a path that visits every grid square exactly once each, spelling them out as it goes. The path can only travel horizontally or vertically between squares. Your path should end at the word 'tit', which is marked in already.

	B	L	O	W	D	M
U	L	L	O	C	E	A
E	W	I	A	I	L	R
L	O	G	L	A	H	S
D	O	N	G	T	C	R
C	L	T	E	T	S	E
R	E	S	D	T	I	T

What Bird Am I?

Where and How Do I Feed in the Garden?

How carefully do you watch the birds in your garden, especially those at your feeders? Can you identify the birds from the descriptions? Write the description number next to the bird.

__. Starling   __. Robin   __. Coal tit

__. Dunnock   __. Tawny owl   __. Magpie

__. Chaffinch   __. Blackbird   __. Greenfinch

__. Goldfinch

1. I feed in groups on the lawn. I probe my bill into the grass. If I use the bird feeders, it's usually the flat table, and I gobble down my food with a complete lack of decorum.

2. I am very tame, and one of my best methods of feeding is to follow the activities of people gardening, often finding creatures displaced by mowing or weeding.

3. I feed on the grass, running for a while and then stopping to look and listen for signs of my favourite food, worms. I also feed from ground feeders and tables. In the autumn, I eat berries.

4. I tend to hog the seed-feeders. In fact, my partner and I often stay for ages, just using the perches and nibbling away at the seeds. When we feed, the husks often fall from our bills. We are happy to eat almost any seeds, even sunflower seeds from heads, but we'll also munch dandelion seeds on the ground.

5. I often feed on the ground, on all sorts of garden insects on the lawn, including leatherjackets, just by walking around and looking. In the breeding season, I occasionally raid the nests of small birds and get a lot of flak for doing so.

6. Sorry to say, I am a frequent victim of bullying at the feeders, usually by my relatives. However, when I do visit I make it quick, darting in and out without being noticed, just taking one seed. The rest of the time I feed in the upper branches of conifers.

7. I sometimes come to feeders, but I am more comfortable on trays or tables. I like to feed on the ground, in flocks, where I walk with a slightly chicken-like shuffle. I have bright white shoulders.

8. Nobody notices me because I feed nocturnally. I eat all sorts of things, including mice and rats, and I attack birds at roosts. I often use streetlights to hunt, dropping down on prey from a height. I sometimes eat worms on lawns.

9. You can hardly see what I'm eating, because my thin bill only allows for small items. I take seeds while shuffling along the ground, and also insects. I often feed on the ground beneath feeders.

10. I come down with my mates in an explosion of colour, and we all love to feed on tiny seeds from feeders, all at once. When this fails, we feed on seed heads, especially thistles and teasel.

Did You Know?

The clutch size of the blue tit is the most variable of any songbird known – it ranges from three to nineteen.

General Knowledge

Colours

Can you remember the colour of these parts of garden birds without looking at a picture?

What colour is/are:

1. The legs of a dunnock

2. The forehead of a robin (feathers above the bill in front of the crown)

3. Head of a black-headed gull in the breeding season

4. Bill of a male blackbird

5. Tail of a blue tit

6. Bill of a greenfinch

7. The base of a male starling's bill in the breeding season

8. The base of a female starling's bill in the breeding season

9. The chin of a male house sparrow

10. The rump (lower back, above tail) of a chaffinch

Answers on page 207

PUZZLE 5

Wordsearch

Find the names of 12 garden birds in this letter grid.
The names can read horizontally, vertically or diagonally,
forwards or backwards.

```
R G Y P S T A R L I N G W D C
E G A C F F R R U L G C S A G
K U L R E F N N E D E N H O O
C E W C P N A O C I O C G P R
E I O H I E G H O E N L I E N
P P R D C C N Y Z I G E F A O
D G R R D N I M F F D S K C E
O A A O N E I N A W X C D G G
O M P B W N E F A R O I E D I
W N S I S E Y G L N G H H D P
N H E N R K T A N L I L P C D
E O S G E A H U J G U E E H O
E O U N I R D D W I O B L R O
R K O L G O L D F I N C H G W
G N H N M H L W E Y P A U E G
```

BULLFINCH	JAY
DUNNOCK	MAGPIE
GOLDFINCH	PIED WAGTAIL
GREENFINCH	ROBIN
GREEN WOODPECKER	STARLING
HOUSE SPARROW	WOODPIGEON

True or False?

	True	False
1. A magpie can recognise itself in the mirror.		
2. A blue tit weighs less than a £2 coin.		
3. The coal tit is the only one of the garden tits that regularly hovers to get food.		
4. The mating of a pair of dunnocks only lasts for a single second.		
5. The bullfinch develops pouches in its mouth in the spring and summer so that it can bring back lots of food for its young.		
6. The swift catches flying insects by opening its mouth and flying through swarms.		
7. Grey herons sometimes eat moles, instead of their usual diet of fish.		
8. The magpie frequently steals shiny objects such as wedding rings.		
9. The loud drumming sound of a great spotted woodpecker is made when the bird is excavating wood.		
10. The nuthatch can walk headfirst both up and down tree trunks.		

PUZZLE 7

General Knowledge

1. What food-procuring trick does a song thrush have that the blackbird is unable to emulate?

2. How can you tell a male great tit from a female by sight?

3. What's the main food in the wild for a goldfinch?

4. Which garden bird is famous for its enormous gatherings on winter nights, involving swirling masses of birds in the sky?

5. What's the main difference between a long-tailed tit's nest compared to nests of other tits?

6. What sort of nest does a woodpigeon make?

7. 'Pie' was the word for magpie before it was a word for a pastry. Do you know what 'pie' referred to?

8. What's the main food that a blue tit brings to its chicks in the nest?

9. Which common garden bird is famous for carrying messages for people?

10. What common garden bird are you most likely to see sunbathing (not while you are sunbathing!)?

Answers on page 208

PUZZLE 8

Fitword

Can you place all these garden birds into the grid, crossword style? Ignore any spaces.

Four-letter word
Wren

Five-letter words
Robin
Serin

Six-letter word
Siskin

Seven-letter word
Jackdaw

Eight-letter words
Blackcap
Starling

Nine-letter word
Chaffinch

Ten-letter words
Greenfinch
Song thrush

Answers on page 208

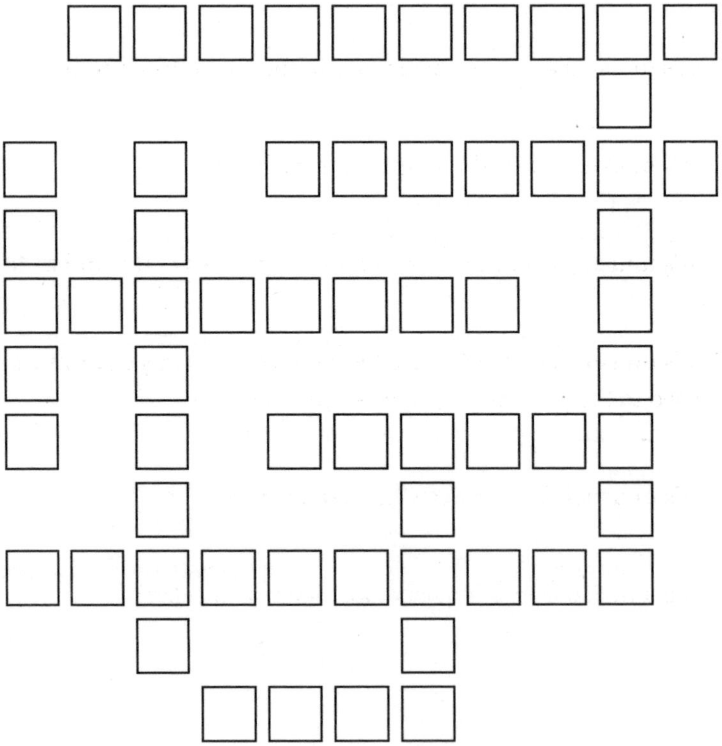

PUZZLE 9

General Knowledge

What's Unusual?

1. What's unusual about the nest-building behaviour of the wren?

2. What's unusual about the song of the wren?

3. What's unusual about the relative sizes of the male and female sparrowhawk?

4. What's unusual about the male and female plumage of the tree sparrow?

5. What's unusual about the behaviour of the jay in the autumn?

6. What's unusual about the song of the starling?

7. What's unusual about the nest-building activities of the nuthatch?

8. What's unusual about a flock of feral pigeons in a city or town, as opposed to the other pigeon species you find there?

9. What's unusual about the nesting habits of robins?

10. What's unusual about the diet of a green woodpecker?

Answers on page 209

PUZZLE 10

Missing Words

A garden watcher's notebook has recently turned up, but its owner spilled some water over it from the bird bath, meaning that some of the words are incomplete. Are you able to fill them in?

1. It was the weekend of the RSPB's _ _ _ Garden Birdwatch. I sat down in my kitchen to watch the comings and goings on the feeders.

2. What I needed to do was to observe my space for a whole _ _ _ _ and count the maximum number of each bird that I saw.

3. I am lucky that I have plenty of _ _ _ _ _ sparrows, and these were the first birds that I saw.

4. This morning, there were plenty of gulls _ _ _ _ _ _ _ _ _ _ but I couldn't count these, because birds only qualify if they land.

5. While I was watching the feeders, a predatory _ _ _ _ _ _ _ _ _ _ _ _ made a rush at the feeders, hoping for a snack, but all the tits and finches got away.

6. One of the annoying things with this survey is that many bird rascals came along _ _ _ _ _ _ _ _ _ and gorged themselves, but haven't turned up today.

7. It's not as if I don't put out enough food for them. I practically bankrupt myself buying black _ _ _ _ _ _ _ _ _ seeds.

8. And I'm very careful with bird hygiene. I always use 'no _ _ _ _' seed mixes so that less spills on the ground.

9. I was very excited to see some _ _ _ _ _ _ _ _ _ _ _ _ because they have suffered a great deal in this area from a horrible disease called Trichomonosis.

10. But in the end, the best bird of the day had nothing to do with the feeders. It was a grey _ _ _ _ _ _ _ trotting around at the edge of the pond.

General Knowledge

Tits

1. Which of the British tits is the most numerous in the UK?

2. Which of the British tits strangely nests in parts of Scotland, is completely absent from all of England and Wales, yet breeds in France?

3. Which two British tits were once thought of as the same species?

4. Which two British birds called 'tit' by name, are not particularly closely related to all the rest?

5. Which tit is famous for having a vast number of different calls, so much so that birdwatchers sometimes say: 'If you don't know what it is, it's a . . .'?

6. What adaptation allows the tits to perform acrobatics in the treetops when feeding?

7. Famously, how many caterpillars can two parent tits bring to their young each day?

8. Which British tit is occasionally predatory on more than just insects? It has been known to eat both small birds and bats!

9. Which British tit sometimes nests in old mouse holes on the ground?

10. Which British tit is particularly adapted to feeding in the very tops of deciduous trees such as oaks?

Crossword

Across

3. These facial features are white on a great tit (6)

5. Pattern of a goldcrest's yellow marking (6)

6. Colour seen in a starling's plumage (6)

8. Red part of a male robin (5)

9. General name for a bird's melodious call (4)

10. Colourful crow-family member (3)

12. Sound typically made by a pigeon (3)

13. Loud and raucous, like a magpie (5)

15. Magpie body part that is noticeably long (4)

16. A carrion crow's dominant colour (5)

17. The collared species of this bird is common in Britain (4)

18. Simple structure often used for feeding birds in a garden (5)

Down

1. This variety of warbler is not often seen in its namesake (6)

2. Characteristic pattern seen on a starling's plumage (5)

4. Spending most of its time alone, like a dunnock (8)

5. The opposite of 4 down, like a starling (6)

6. A type of bird often found in cities (6)

7. Vivid colour found on a goldfinch's face (3)

11. Bright colour found on a greenfinch's wings (6)

12. Intelligent, like a carrion crow (6)

14. Diminutive, like a wren (5)

15. Type of common songbird (3)

PUZZLE 13

Multiple Choice

Garden Bird Voices

The garden is the best place to start learning bird voices – you will hear birds in your back yard, even if you don't want to. See if you can match the bird to the description of its voice.

1. A loud, mischievous chatter

   a. *Magpie*　　　**b.** *Carrion crow*

   c. *Nuthatch*　　**d.** *Dunnock*

2. A cheerful, bell-like song 'teacher, teacher, teacher'

   a. *Starling*　　**b.** *Blue tit*

   c. *Chaffinch*　　**d.** *Great tit*

3. A cheerful 'pink-pink' to go with the breast colour

   a. *Chaffinch*　　**b.** *Greenfinch*

   c. *Goldfinch*　　**d.** *Bullfinch*

4. A loud, clear song, repeating every phrase several times before going on to the next: 'he sings each song twice over, lest you think he never could recapture that first fine careless rapture' (Robert Browning)

   a. *Blackbird*　　**b.** *Song thrush*

   c. *Robin*　　　**d.** *Collared dove*

5. A dreary cooing dirge of three repeated notes: 'U – ni – ted'

   a. *Robin*　　　　**b.** *Woodpigeon*

   c. *Collared dove*　**d.** *Tawny owl*

6. A babbling, madcap medley often sung from a roof aerial, often including much mimicry

   a. *Rook*　　　**b.** *Collared dove*

   c. *Blackbird*　　**d.** *Starling*

7. A very loud, angry 'caw' often delivered three times in succession

   a. *Magpie*　　**b.** *Jackdaw*

   c. *Carrion crow*　**d.** *Jay*

8. A very varied, quite gentle, wistful song with long pauses, often sung on winter nights

   a. *Robin*　　　**b.** *Chaffinch*

   c. *Blackbird*　　**d.** *Great tit*

9. An unimpressive range of tweet and cheep calls, made in conversational manner

   a. *Bullfinch*　　**b.** *House sparrow*

   c. *Starling*　　**d.** *Feral pigeon*

10. Short, bubbly calls, with an embarrassing similarity to quiet flatulence!

    a. *Great tit*　　**b.** *Starling*

    c. *Tawny owl*　　**d.** *House martin*

Answers on page 210

PUZZLE 14

Word Ladder

Complete each of these word ladders by writing a regular English word at each step. Each word must use the exact same letters in the same order as the word above, except with a single letter changed.

For example:

SHOW > SHOT > SOOT > SORT > SORE > MORE

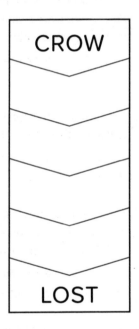

CROW

LOST

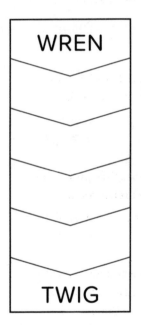

WREN

TWIG

Did You Know?

A bird's visible 'knees' are actually
its ankles.

General Knowledge

Sleeping Arrangements

As dusk falls, the bustle of the garden dies down – or does it?
The sleeping arrangements of our neighbourhood birds are
often as interesting as their daytime behaviour.
What do you know about them?

1. Which garden bird is famous for sleeping on the wing?

2. Which garden bird doesn't sleep at night?

3. Which garden bird makes an infernal racket as it beds down, with nearby birds making angry 'chink' calls?

4. When it is very cold, which normally unsociable garden birds will gather in a hole and huddle in bodily contact?

5. Which garden bird often sings in cities at night, because it is quieter then and it can be heard?

6. Which garden bird sleeps at night huddling together with family members?

7. Which birds sleep in trees and make a loud rustle and kerfuffle when they are disturbed?

8. Which garden bird may travel up to 50 km (31 miles) to join a large communal roost?

9. Which common neighbourhood bird often gathers with its own species in odd places such as garage roofs, greenhouses and Christmas tree lights?

10. Which common neighbourhood bird tends to go to the sea or to large lakes to roost?

Answers on page 211

PUZZLE 16

True or False?

Robins

How much do you know about Britain's favourite bird?
Work out whether these statements are true or false.

	True	False
1. One study found that ten per cent of all adult male robins are killed by other robins.		
2. The robin is only unofficially Britain's National Bird; the government has never confirmed it.		
3. One of its closest relatives is the American robin of the USA.		
4. The robin often sings at night and is mistaken for a nightingale.		
5. The robin has larger eyes than most small birds and, as a result, often sings earlier in the dawn chorus than other species.		
6. Female robins don't sing often, if at all.		
7. Robins don't migrate.		
8. It is thought that robins are tame around gardeners because, back in the distant past, they used to follow large mammals around to gather insects flushed out by their movements.		
9. Unusually, the male robin builds most of the nest.		
10. The robin has a large clutch of eggs, regularly nine to ten.		

Answers on page 211

Word Circle

Rearrange the letters in the circle below to reveal a bird that's well-known for its mellow song. Then, how many other words can you find that use the centre letter plus two or more of the other letters? No letter may be used more times than it appears within the circle. These words also include two other birds.

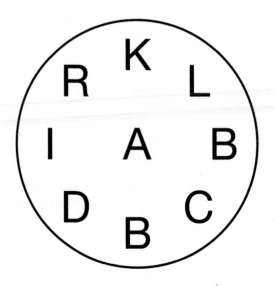

Mix and Match

Garden Birds and Their Nests

Can you match the garden bird with its style of nest?

A remarkable, domed nest made from moss and cobwebs, with lichen on the outside and 800–2,000 feathers stuffed inside.

A large, domed structure of twigs, placed in the branches of a tree, sometimes quite low down.

WOODPIGEON

HOUSE MARTIN

A shallow depression on the ground, made from grass and lined with the female's breast feathers.

GREAT TIT

A platform of twigs in a shrub or tree, so poorly constructed you can see the eggs from below.

LONG-TAILED TIT

A cup of mud attached to a vertical surface, often under the eaves of buildings.

GOLDFINCH

A very neat cup, woven with grass and moss and lined with copious plant down, often thistledown, placed towards the end of a tree or shrub branch.

CARRION CROW

MAGPIE

A chamber in a tree, excavated by the parents, with no lining except for some chippings.

HOUSE SPARROW

Often a bit of a mess, an unruly dome of grass in a bush or stuffed into a nest box, sometimes also a house martin nest.

GREAT SPOTTED
WOODPECKER

A large cup of twigs and earth, placed high up in the upper branches of a tree.

MALLARD

A cup made mostly out of moss, lined with grass and often feathers, placed inside a hole, often a nest box.

PUZZLE 19

What Bird Am I?

The following statements are all true of one common garden bird.
What is it?

1. I am the smallest member of my family in Britain, and that can cause me trouble.

2. I am most at home in conifer woods, but outside the breeding season I can be found in all kinds of woodland, as well as gardens.

3. I am one of the few garden birds that regularly hovers, up in the trees.

4. To avoid aggression, I often snatch food quickly away from the feeding station, and then store it away in a quiet place for later consumption.

5. In common with most of my family, I have a remarkable dietary change season to season – insects in spring and summer, but mainly nuts and seeds in autumn and winter.

6. In contrast to the rest of my family, I often try two broods in a season.

7. My usual clutch is nine to ten eggs.

8. I nest in a hole in a tree, or a nest box.

9. I am not very faithful to my partner!

10. I often feed on the ground, as well as up in the trees.

PUZZLE 20

Codeword

Solve the following codeword and then rearrange the shaded squares to reveal a bird that might visit a garden. A codeword is a coded crossword in which every letter has been replaced by a number, indicated by the small digits in the top left corner of each crossword square.

As a further clue, the puzzle also contains two more birds that might visit a garden. Other words, however, are not bird-related.

	N
A	21 · 15 · 21 · 23 · 13 · 2 · 5 · · 8 · 10 · 23 · 12
B	22 P · 4 · · 19 · · 4 · · · 6 · · 26 · O
C	25 · 21 · 19 · 5 · 10 · 12 · 23 · · 12 · 13 · 23 · 10 · 11 · P
D	21 · · 4 · · 10 · · 13 · · 22 · · 19 · · 12 · Q
E	7 · 18 · 2 · 13 · 7 · · 24 · 19 · 21 · 3 · 10 · 12 · · R
F	13 · · · · 19 · · 18 · · 19 · · 3 · · 7 · S
G	2 · 21 · 9 · 13 · 10 · 12 · · 24 · 19 · 10 · 10 · 17 · 10 · T
H	5 · · 13 · · 10 · · 26 · · 4 · · · · · 2 · U
I	· 7 · 4 · 26 · 22 · 4 O · 2 · · 14 · 10 · 10 · 1 · 12 · V
J	12 · · 25 · · 10 · · 13 · · 16 · · 21 · · 4 · W
K	7 · 16 · 21 · 13 · 19 · · 20 · 26 · 21 · 19 · 23 · 10 · 19 · X
L	26 · · 23 · · · 26 · · 14 · · 13 · · 12 · Y
M	11 · 13 · 10 · 12 · · 12 · 10 · 10 · 1 · 13 · 2 · 5 G · Z

1	2	3	4	5	6	7	8	9	10	11	12	13

14	15	16	17	18	19	20	21	22	23	24	25	26

PUZZLE 21

General Knowledge

Finches

1. Which small garden finch with greenish-yellow wing-bars first turned up in gardens in the 1960s and has a habit of feeding upside down?

2. Which garden finch is unusual for being very quiet and shy?

3. Which attractive finch with an orange wash to its plumage is a winter visitor to Britain in varying numbers each year, depending on the availability of beech mast?

4. Which garden finch generally prefers soft fruits to seeds, especially in the breeding season?

5. Which garden finch has the longest tail?

6. Which garden finch is particularly associated with nyjer seed, although now it is also a fanatic of sunflower hearts?

7. How can you tell a juvenile bullfinch from an adult?

8. Which garden finch is able to eat yew seeds, despite the fact that the berries are deadly poisonous to us?

9. How can you tell the difference between an adult and a juvenile goldfinch?

10. Which garden finch is, unlike many a garden resident, a fan of leylandii?

CHAPTER TWO

BIRD BEHAVIOUR

Mix and Match

Looking for Love?

All of us hope to find love in our lives, but the task is made easier for certain birds by physical features or qualities of the opposite sex. Can you match the wooing features with the species of bird?

HOUSE SPARROW	A 'badge' of black on the chin
BLACKCAP	The size of the white forehead
SWALLOW	The ultraviolet on the crown
BLUE TIT	The length and symmetry of the tail
GREENFINCH	Nest-building prowess
WREN	The spurs on the legs
COOT	The intensity of yellow in the wings
PHEASANT	An ability to catch and bring fish
SEDGE WARBLER	The density of vegetation in the territory
COMMON TERN	The repertoire in the song

Fitword

Can you place all these bird calls into the grid, crossword style?
Ignore any spaces or punctuation.

Four-letter words
Karr
Ow ow
Wink

Five-letter words
Huitt
Waruk

Six-letter words
Chreee
Crrrib
Hoo hoo
Kweooo
Oop oop
Tchack
Terric
Zip-zap

Seven-letter words
Chirrup
Cook-roo

Eight-letter words
Took took
Wiwwierr
Zeee-zeee

Nine-letter words
Ark ark ark
Yikkering

True or False?

Bird Sounds

	True	False
1. Chaffinch songs have dialects and experts can tell where a singing bird is from.		
2. Although it nests on the ground, the skylark only ever sings in the air.		
3. Starlings are known to mimic all kinds of sounds, including car alarms.		
4. The booming sound of the bittern is the most far-carrying of British bird sounds, audible from 2 km (1¼ miles).		
5. The dawn chorus lasts for several hours in spring.		
6. Different species of birds often make similar calls to announce the presence of a predator, carrying the message to the bird community at large.		
7. Songbirds often learn their song from their father and his neighbours.		
8. The reed bunting changes its song when it pairs up.		
9. Birds tend to sing when they are happy and joyful.		
10. The cuckoo changes its tune in June.		

Answers on page 215

Word Circle

Rearrange the letters in the circle below to reveal a term that describes the 'wink-wink' call of the pink-footed goose.

Then, how many other words can you find that use the centre letter plus two or more of the other letters? No letter may be used more times than it appears within the circle.

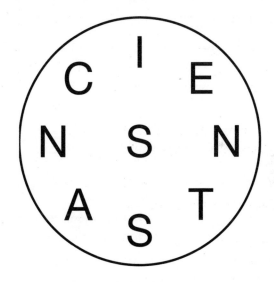

Who Am I?

Parenting

The following sentences describe the way in which the species looks after its young. Can you work out the species? To help you, we've included the number of letters in the answer.

1. I don't feed or look after my young. I let someone else do it.

— — — — — —

2. I always have two young. I eat grain and convert it in my crop to a kind of milk that my young drink. People never recognise my young as such.

— — — — — — — — —

3. I spend much of the high summer days catching flying insects on the wing for my chicks. Sometimes, if the weather is bad, I have to fly a long way away, so I am delayed bringing food. But my chicks are adapted to that.

— — — — —

4. I hide my nest away as best as I can, but almost as soon as my young hatch I have to lead them to water. This can involve crossing gardens, parks and public places, even roads. Sometimes the traffic has to stop for me as I lead the cheeping convoy.

— — — — — — —

5. Feeding young is exhausting for me. As soon as they hatch, all I do all day is look for caterpillars. I time my breeding to the glut of caterpillars. When I deliver these insects, I break their jaw with my beak so that they don't bite my nestlings.

— — — — — — — —

6. I have only one hungry chick. I have to fly far out to sea to find fish for it, and when I return, I carry these fish dangling from my bill.

— — — — — —

7. My young like nothing better than earthworms. I spend hours looking for these on the garden lawn, running back and forth, stopping every so often to look and listen. My young eat other invertebrates, too.

— — — — — — — —

8. I do all the food shopping for the family. Sometimes I have more than one family to feed. I catch prey, mainly birds and mammals, for one or two nests, sometimes even more. The fun part is that, on my return towards the nest, the female comes up to have a fly around and I drop the offering from my talons to hers.

— — — — —   — — — — — —

9. I am often seen on ponds and ditches going back and forth to my chicks, which are a fluffy, coal-black with dishevelled red hair, looking like big bumblebees. We swim together and I feed them beak-to-beak.

— — — —

10. I catch fish and take them to my treetop nest, where my young squabble for them.

— — — —   — — — — —

Answers on page 215

Multiple Choice

Unusual Behaviour

Test your knowledge on the many remarkable and
unusual things that birds do.

1. Which bird, gruesomely, impales its prey on thorns or branches and
stores it here?

   a. *Shrike*   **b.** *Sparrowhawk*

   c. *Merlin*   **d.** *Kingfisher*

2. The cuckoo is known for laying its own eggs in other nests, and letting other
birds raise them, but can you name another, non-cuckoo brood parasite?

   a. *Blue tit*   **b.** *Moorhen*

   c. *Blackbird*   **d.** *Little egret*

3. Several British birds are known for the males gathering on communal
display grounds, known as 'leks'. Can you name one of them?

   a. *Peregrine*   **b.** *Pheasant*

   c. *Black grouse*   **d.** *House sparrow*

4. Gulls have a curious habit of trampling their feet in puddles. What is the
reason for this?

   a. *It is part of the courtship display*

   b. *It helps to wash their feet*

   c. *It keeps them fit*

   d. *It may bring worms to the surface*

5. What insects do birds sometimes collect in their bill and appear to apply to
the surface of their plumage?

   a. *Ants*   **b.** *Earwigs*

   c. *Ladybirds*   **d.** *Midges*

6. What unusual 'ingredient' do great crested grebes sometimes use during their courtship display?

   a. *Fish*   **b.** *Feathers*

   c. *Water weed*   **d.** *Sticks*

7. And what delightful and unusual gesture of parental care do these species share: great crested grebe, mute swan, tufted duck?

   a. *The adults pick the young chicks up in their bills*

   b. *The young form creches*

   c. *The young help each other to feed*

   d. *The parents carry young chicks on their back*

8. Several waders have a special method of protecting their eggs or young when a predator is near, which involves deception. What do they do?

   a. *They pretend to have a broken wing*

   b. *They pretend to be a rodent*

   c. *They pretend to incubate somewhere else*

   d. *They pretend to be busy*

9. What delightful and very special way do several raptors, notably harriers, have to transfer prey from one parent to another when feeding young?

   a. *They place food at a collection point*

   b. *They bring food to the nest*

   c. *They exchange food*

   d. *They use a mid-air food pass*

10. What is the main way in which a grey heron procures its fishy food?

   a. *It wades in the water and then grabs a fish at its feet*

   b. *It dives in from a height*

   c. *It grabs fish with its feet*

   d. *It jumps in from the banks of the river or lake*

Answers on page 215

Mix and Match

Match the species to the number of eggs in its average clutch.

PUFFIN	6
COLLARED DOVE	9
COMMON GULL	1
DUNLIN	8
HEN HARRIER	7
MOORHEN	5
GOLDCREST	10+
MARSH TIT	4
BLUE TIT	2
PHEASANT	3

PUZZLE 29

Codeword

Solve the following codeword and then rearrange the shaded squares to reveal a word that can be used to describe any bird at some point in its life. A codeword is a coded crossword in which every letter has been replaced by a number, indicated by the small digits in the top left corner of each crossword square.

As a further clue, the puzzle also contains two words that describe in turn a bird behaviour, and what the result might be. Other words, however, are not bird-related.

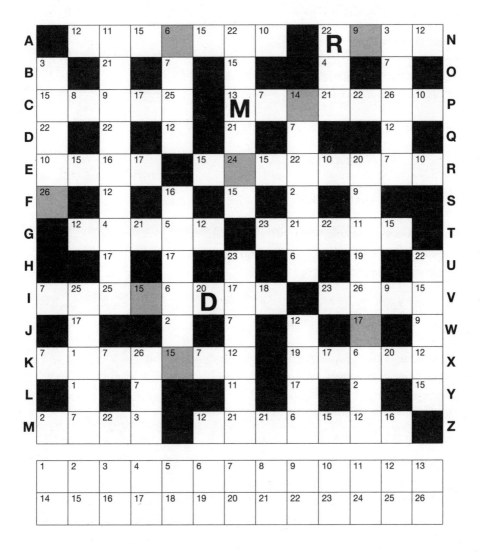

True or False?

Males and Females

It takes two to tango and, usually, to try a breeding attempt. Test your knowledge here about the different roles of males and females.

	True	False
1. In the breeding season, the male sex organs of a ruff are heavier than its brain.		
2. In most British birds, it is primarily the role of the female to incubate the eggs.		
3. In almost all British birds, the male is ultimately responsible for choosing whether a pair will form or not.		
4. The song of a male stimulates a female to get into breeding condition.		
5. Male birds tend to have more colourful and bolder plumage than females.		
6. Some female birds take a break, or 'holiday', before starting the business of breeding.		
7. Most male birds have a penis that is concealed within the body feathering until use.		
8. Both males and females routinely sing during the breeding season.		
9. Birds sometimes form homosexual pairs.		
10. Males often bring food to their mates, delivering it bill-to-bill, and this is known as courtship feeding.		

Answers on page 217

PUZZLE 31

General Knowledge
'Terms and Conditions'

1. When does a bird usually start incubating – after the first egg is laid, or after the last is laid?

2. Apart from keeping eggs warm and protecting them, what else must an incubating adult do?

3. What is the term for a complete set of youngsters?

4. What is each hatched youngster called within a nest?

5. And then what is it called when it leaves the nest?

6. What general term is used for a fluffy youngster that isn't confined to a nest but sometimes also for youngsters in a nest, too?

7. What is the term for the loud noises that young birds make when demanding food from the parent?

8. What is the term for a parent bird sitting on young birds to keep them warm, as opposed to eggs?

9. What is a young swan called?

10. What is a young bird called when it has its first complete set of feathers?

Answers on page 217

Pathfinder

Can you find six birds, all known for their skulking, in the grid below? Starting at the shaded square, find a path that visits every grid square exactly once each, spelling them out as it goes. The path can only travel horizontally or vertically between squares.

All of the birds have two-word names, bar one. The bird with a one-word name is especially tricky to spot when skulking. What is it?

	S	H	W	A	L	E	R
W	R	A	M	R	B	I	N
A	T	E	T	I	T	G	H
A	R	R	E	A	T	I	T
I	A	K	R	I	C	N	G
L	R	E	G	R	E	L	A
S	C	D	E	L	B	U	N
P	O	T	T	G	N	I	T

What Bird Am I?

Can you guess the British bird from these statements?

1. My favourite food is hairy caterpillars.

2. I am usually the first summer visitor to return south after breeding, often leaving Britain by June and arriving in Africa by July.

3. These days I am more common in the north of the country.

4. Between the early 1980s and 2022, I declined by 65 per cent.

5. I am very difficult to see, but very easy to hear.

6. When flying, my wings distinctively don't rise above the horizontal.

7. I never knowingly meet my parents.

8. I am the scourge of reed warblers, meadow pipits and dunnocks.

9. I am a killer before I even fledge the nest.

10. If female, I may lay 20 eggs in a season.

Answers on page 217

General Knowledge

Nests and Eggs

1. What term is often used to describe an eagle's nest?

2. What shape are most birds' eggs, and why?

3. What tends to be characteristic of eggs laid in holes and cavities?

4. What is particularly unusual about the markings on a guillemot's egg?

5. What do you call a colony of heron nests?

6. And a colony of rooks?

7. And a colony of cormorants?

8. What very unusual trick do female starlings sometimes play on their neighbours?

9. What useful anatomical feature do chicks have to help them hatch?

10. What do many female birds eat in the stages leading up to egg formation?

Wordsearch

Bird Habits

Find the names of 24 bird habits hidden in this letter grid.
The names can read horizontally, vertically or diagonally,
forwards or backwards.

S	D	I	V	E	O	N	A	H	N	T	D	D	A	R
S	S	Y	N	U	P	T	S	H	I	I	S	D	G	I
N	E	S	T	R	U	A	C	E	S	O	V	O	E	A
T	A	P	E	R	D	U	D	P	L	E	S	E	O	P
R	R	E	T	E	O	E	L	I	R	M	R	L	H	R
E	N	S	E	R	F	A	A	T	R	E	F	B	N	L
V	E	S	C	E	Y	H	I	M	H	U	U	M	C	F
O	R	T	N	I	A	S	O	T	B	D	L	U	C	H
H	L	D	U	E	E	A	A	B	E	U	U	T	L	F
B	M	A	O	H	C	G	S	E	A	O	S	A	A	L
E	E	T	A	B	U	C	N	I	Y	S	N	H	M	O
C	A	A	T	Y	V	S	T	N	R	L	B	E	B	C
N	L	E	V	E	H	E	L	T	T	U	C	S	E	K
A	C	V	R	R	P	T	Y	L	F	R	H	A	R	H
D	E	M	I	G	R	A	T	E	F	E	E	D	F	D

ADVERTISE	DIVE	MIGRATE
AMBUSH	EAT	NEST
CLAMBER	FEED	PAIR
CROUCH	FLOCK	PREEN
DANCE	FLY	ROOST
DASH	GATHER	SCUTTLE
DEFEND	HOVER	STRUT
DISPLAY	INCUBATE	TUMBLE

Multiple Choice
Bird Songs and Calls

Can you guess the sound from the description? To help, you can choose from the four options.

1. Delightful tinkling calls with a merry tone, sounding like 'tickle it'.

   a. *Magpie*   **b.** *Goldfinch*

   c. *Swallow*   **d.** *Blue tit*

2. Its noisiest sounds are made by the wings, which make a beautiful sighing melody. Also snorts.

   a. *Chaffinch*   **b.** *Canada goose*

   c. *Golden eagle* **d.** *Mute swan*

3. The song is famous for its length and intensity, sounding like a commentator describing a 100m race. It is always sung from low down.

   a. *Chaffinch*   **b.** *Wren*

   c. *Goldcrest*   **d.** *Long-tailed tit*

4. A curious shriek, in keeping with the bird's somewhat mysterious nature.

   a. *Barn owl*   **b.** *Great crested grebe*

   c. *Mallard*   **d.** *Rook*

5. A far-carrying and deep 'kronk'

   a. *Wren*   **b.** *Red grouse*

   c. *Cuckoo*   **d.** *Raven*

6. The loud coughing is one of the sounds of the countryside. In spring the male simultaneously flaps its wings.

   a. *Herring gull* **b.** *Greylag goose*

   c. *Pheasant*   **d.** *Whooper swan*

7. Main call is 'cour-li', while the song is a glorious ecstatic bubbling trill.

   a. *Whitethroat*   **b.** *Curlew*

   c. *Nightjar*   **d.** *Hobby*

8. An excited 'whee-ooo' from males in winter flocks. The females grunt.

   a. *Woodpigeon*   **b.** *Wigeon*

   c. *Carrion crow* **d.** *Cuckoo*

9. A far-carrying bugling.

   a. *Crane*   **b.** *Spoonbill*

   c. *Coot*   **d.** *Raven*

10. A shrill scream, often made by groups flying closely together around buildings.

    a. *Golden eagle* **b.** *Swift*

    c. *Curlew*   **d.** *Jay*

Answers on page 218

Mix and Match

Flocks

How much do you know about the sociability of our birds?
Who nests singly away from others of their kind, who nests in
a colony, or who does neither one nor the other?

Put the species in the appropriate category.

KINGFISHER   GOLDFINCH   HOUSE SPARROW

LAPWING   KITTIWAKE   BLACK-HEADED GULL

AVOCET   HOUSE MARTIN   ROBIN

FIELDFARE

Large colony	Small colony	Informal clumping of pairs	Territorial (nests singly)

Crossword

Across

2. Berry, perhaps; type of food eaten by redwings in autumn (5)

7. Found in water; a rare species of warbler (7)

9. An eater of everything, like a rook (8)

10. Food item responsible for part of the name of *Sitta europaea* (3)

11. Maize, perhaps; type of field where skylarks feed (6)

14. Compact plant growth, often eaten by woodpigeons (3)

15. Grasslike plant for which *Acrocephalus schoenobaenus* is named (5)

17. Plant's underground support, sometimes eaten by water rails (4)

18. Example of 11 across, used in bread-making and eaten by stock doves (5)

19. Small mammal, eaten by e.g. owls (4)

20. Common garden white-petalled flower, eaten by e.g. some geese (5)

Down

1. The seeds produced by 11 across (5)

3. Spiny sea echinoderm sometimes eaten by eider (6)

4. Frog larva, sometimes eaten by wrens (7)

5. Feed on grassland, like a brent goose (5)

6. Mollusc with a purple shell, eaten by turnstones (6)

8. Oak-tree produce, eaten by jays (5)

12. Waterside plant with stalk-like leaves, often used for nest building (4)

13. Simple, typically aquatic plants that may be single-celled, eaten by ducks (5)

14. Example of 11 across; type of field where quail may live (6)

15. A plant's stalk, eaten by Canada geese (4)

16. Plunge down into water, like a duck might (4)

18. A self-seeded, unwanted plant (4)

Mix and Match

Can you tally the bird to its feeding habits?

CHOUGH	Ants, beetles and other invertebrates
DARTFORD WARBLER	Medium sized birds and mammals
WATER RAIL	Insects, especially their larvae
GOSHAWK	Berries, seeds, shoots
RED-THROATED DIVER	Worms and other invertebrates
	Insects and other invertebrates
PTARMIGAN	Eats almost anything, even young birds
CETTI'S WARBLER	
WHEATEAR	Insects and spiders
	Fish
DIPPER	
COMMON SNIPE	Insects

Word Ladder

Complete each of these word ladders by writing a regular English word at each step. Each word must use the exact same letters in the same order as the word above, except with a single letter changed.

For example,

SHOW > SHOT > SOOT > SORT > SORE > MORE

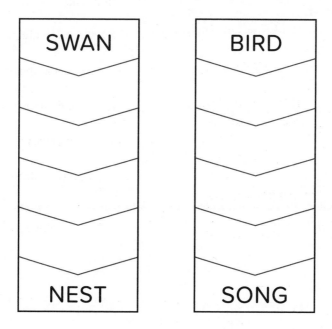

SWAN

NEST

BIRD

SONG

Multiple Choice

Displays and Courtship

Our birds perform some splendid displays to make sure that their mates are suitably impressed with them, but do you know which bird makes the display described?

1. It approaches its partner on the water and shakes its head. Often it dips its bill towards its back and pretends to preen. Then it dives down and gathers water weed.

   a. *Puffin*

   b. *Great crested grebe*

   c. *Mallard*

   d. *Coot*

2. It swims on the water, then suddenly looks up with its neck extended, as if pointing at the sky. It might lift its rear end, too.

   a. *Red-breasted merganser*

   b. *Herring gull*

   c. *Guillemot*

   d. *Mute swan*

3. It takes off from a high perch and begins a curious fluttering flight, like that of a swallow, describing a wide circle or figure of eight at the same height, singing all the while.

   a. *House martin*

   b. *Spotted flycatcher*

   c. *Greenfinch*

   d. *Dunnock*

4. It takes off and flies up in a straight line, then suddenly stops, with a clap of the wings as if shot, and glides down to a new perch.

   a. *Collared dove*

   b. *Cuckoo*

   c. *Curlew*

   d. *Woodpigeon*

5. It flies up from an elevated perch at a steep angle, then glides down, singing all the while, with its wings held steady and tail up, like a paper aeroplane, before landing on the same or another perch.

   a. *Tree pipit*

   b. *Skylark*

   c. *Rock pipit*

   d. *Chaffinch*

6. It flies up from a low perch and after a few metres, singing its scratchy song, it hangs in the air with some effort, as if suspended by elastic.

   a. *Blue tit*
   b. *Chiffchaff*
   c. *Ringed plover*
   d. *Whitethroat*

7. It selects a slight bump in the ground and, lifting its head up, makes a loud coughing sound, at the same time beating its wings.

   a. *Nightjar*
   b. *Pheasant*
   c. *Swift*
   d. *Herring gull*

8. Taking off from a high perch, it flies up to some considerable height, then dives down with wings closed, almost as if it will hit the ground, before opening its wings and using its momentum to rise up again – then to repeat the performance.

   a. *Kestrel*
   b. *Skylark*
   c. *Buzzard*
   d. *Collared dove*

9. It flies not very high above its territory and then proceeds to fly back and forth, ducking and diving and veering from side to side, with throbbing wings and loud melancholy cries.

   a. *Nightjar*
   b. *Swift*
   c. *Black-headed gull*
   d. *Lapwing*

10. It has no display at all.

   a. *Mute swan*
   b. *Song thrush*
   c. *House sparrow*
   d. *Great spotted woodpecker*

Answers on page 221

True or False?

Self-care

How much do you know about how birds look after themselves? Take this true or false quiz to find out.

	True	False
1. Allopreening, when a bird preens another, is so called because a bird is easily able to say 'allo' when close up.		
2. A blackbird needs five baths a day.		
3. Sunbathing, or sunning, is good for a bird's feathers.		
4. Birds often bathe in foliage after rain.		
5. Birds occasionally take small flies up in their bills and rub the insects' bodies over their plumage.		
6. In the autumn, birds sometimes take the juice of berries and rub this over their plumage.		
7. Swallows and swifts skim down to the water surface of a pool or stream and wet their feathers, like a sort of aerial bath.		
8. Birds occasionally bathe in the smoke from chimneys.		
9. Birds bathe in dust in dry places when there is no water for bathing.		
10. Herons have special powder-like plumage that absorbs fish oil.		

Answers on page 221

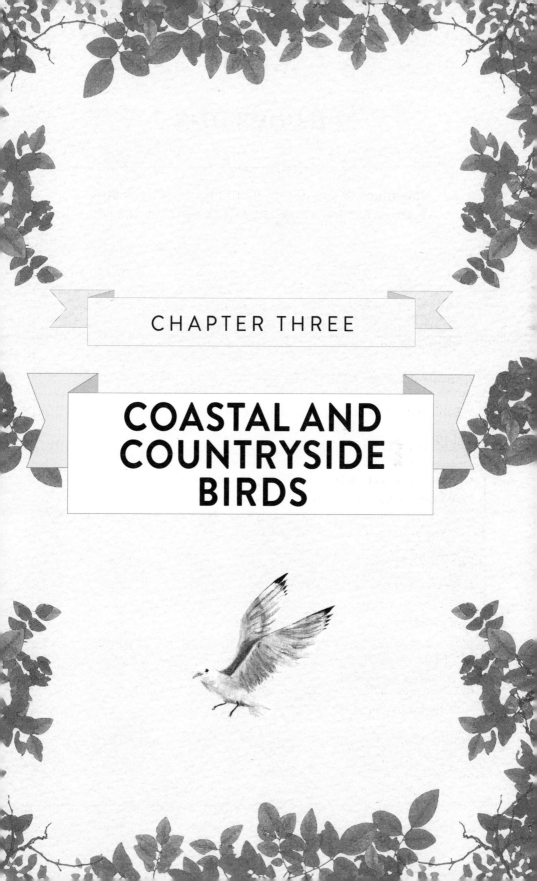

CHAPTER THREE

COASTAL AND COUNTRYSIDE BIRDS

PUZZLE 43

Anagrams

Can you work out any of these species from their anagrams?

1. I am nose hurt

————— ———————

2. The slower road

—————-—————— ———

3. But I'll make clog

————— ——————————

4. Snapped in rom-com

——————— —————————

5. Larger bad wren

—————— ————————

6. With nerd scan

————————— —————

7. Love ladder co

————————— —————

8. Ted a bit red

———————— ———

9. He writes short tale

—————— ——————————————

10. The cat's on

——————————

General Knowledge

1. What, if anything, is inaccurate about the name 'bearded tit'?

2. What's unusual about the feeding habits of skuas?

3. What connects a tit, a harrier and a warbler?

4. Which birds have shock absorbing tissue between the base of their bill and skull?

5. What species inspired the design of Japanese bullet trains?

6. What British bird has a song often rendered, 'a little bit of bread and no cheese'?

7. What's unusual about the nest of a grebe?

8. What is Britain's smallest day-flying bird of prey?

9. What word is typically used to describe the strange nocturnal advertising call of the nightjar?

10. What popular British bird is famous for its ability to carry multiple fish in its colourful bill at the same time?

Pathfinder

The names of seven birds you might spot in the countryside can be uncovered in the grid below by creating a path that starts at the shaded square and moves to each square in turn, spelling out the names. Your path should visit every square, never cross itself, and only move vertically or horizontally. Your path should end back at the shaded square, as though you have gone on a looped walk – though your final move will have to be a diagonal one.

All of the birds are birds of prey, except one. Which one?

K	E	S	E	L	B	U
A	W	T	R	A	Z	Z
H	G	L	W	R	D	M
S	O	N	O	N	I	E
L	L	R	A	P	L	R
A	O	W	B	E	R	E
W	S	E	N	I	R	G

PUZZLE 46

True or False?

	True	False
1. The crossbill's lower mandible can cross the upper mandible either to the right or the left. So, a crossbill is either left-billed or right-billed.		
2. The mute swan is so named because it is unable to make any sounds.		
3. A scarecrow is designed to frighten carrion crows away from crops on farmers' fields.		
4. Oystercatchers are divided into two guilds, each of which specialises in feeding in a particular way.		
5. The rock pipit is the only songbird in Britain that sometimes eats fish.		
6. The lesser black-backed gull is smaller than a great black-backed gull but bigger than a herring gull.		
7. There are more pairs of herring gulls in Britain than puffins (as of 2022).		
8. Measured against all its other activities, a grey heron spends the majority of its average day doing nothing at all.		
9. Seabirds become sick from drinking sea water.		
10. An average female cuckoo will lay its eggs in the nests of several species of small, insectivorous birds.		

Answers on page 223

PUZZLE 47

Codeword

Solve the following codeword and then rearrange the shaded squares to reveal a common North Atlantic auk. A codeword is a coded crossword in which every letter has been replaced by a number, indicated by the small digits in the top left corner of each crossword square.

As a further clue, the puzzle also contains four possible bird habitats.

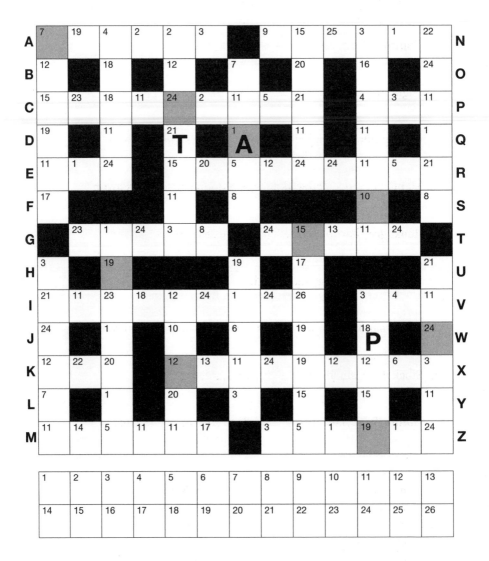

PUZZLE 48

Odd One Out

Can you pick the odd one out among these groups of four birds and explain the reason why? These are particularly tricky, so there are clues below if you need a little help.

1. Mallard, tufted duck, shoveler, pintail

2. Common tern, red kite, swallow, long-tailed tit

3. Nightjar, tawny owl, stone-curlew, turnstone

4. Black guillemot, red kite, white stork, white-tailed eagle

5. Mandarin duck, collared dove, Egyptian goose, black swan

6. Rook, grey heron, Sandwich tern, little egret

7. Coot, blackbird, raven, chough

8. Green sandpiper, green woodpecker, greenfinch, willow warbler

9. Stock dove, shelduck, blue tit, long-tailed tit

10. Dunnock, skylark, meadow pipit, common whitethroat

Clues:

1. Feeding technique	6. Nesting
2. Appearance	7. Colour
3. Activity times	8. Colour
4. Origin of British birds	9. Nesting
5. Origin	10. Singing

Answers on page 224

General Knowledge

1. What is the UK's smallest bird?

2. The Crown claims ownership of which species of bird in the UK?

3. What duck shares its name with a colour?

4. What bird can produce over 1,000 different sounds?

5. What is the UK's smallest owl?

6. What is the fastest flying bird in the UK?

7. What shape do flocks of geese form when flying?

8. What's distinctive about the way a heron flies, especially as opposed to a stork or crane?

9. What is unusual about the ears of a long-eared owl?

10. What rare bird of the reedbeds is famous for making a 'booming' sound?

Wordsearch

Waders

Find the 22 wading birds hidden in this letter grid. The names can read horizontally, vertically or diagonally, forwards or backwards.

```
E  S  E  S  I  G  E  N  O  T  S  N  R  U  T
R  E  R  I  N  G  E  D  P  L  O  V  E  R  A
E  K  N  A  H  S  D  E  R  G  R  N  R  N  L
V  N  I  L  N  U  D  I  N  G  K  E  G  T  I
O  N  G  T  O  N  K  I  R  K  H  L  N  E  T
L  C  O  A  T  H  W  E  C  C  L  D  I  P  T
P  U  D  A  N  P  E  O  T  E  T  O  L  O  L
Y  R  W  I  A  N  C  A  R  E  C  T  R  R  E
E  L  I  L  S  D  C  B  C  F  L  T  E  A  S
R  E  T  H  O  R  M  O  F  E  S  E  D  L  T
G  W  A  O  E  I  V  U  A  S  N  R  N  A  I
S  N  W  T  H  A  R  C  D  N  I  E  A  H  N
K  S  S  W  F  A  O  E  O  N  P  L  S  P  T
R  Y  O  R  E  V  O  L  P  N  E  D  L  O  G
O  T  N  I  T  S  S  K  C  N  I  M  M  E  T
```

AVOCET	KNOT	SANDERLING
CURLEW	LAPWING	SNIPE
DOTTEREL	LITTLE STINT	TEMMINCK'S STINT
DUNLIN	OYSTERCATCHER	TURNSTONE
GODWIT	PHALAROPE	WHIMBREL
GOLDEN PLOVER	REDSHANK	WOODCOCK
GREENSHANK	RINGED PLOVER	
GREY PLOVER	RUFF	

Answers on page 225

What Bird Am I?

Can you recognise each bird from the profile that it might have written itself?

1. I swim regularly but don't dive. I am largely dark but have unexpected red garters and my bill is an unusual combination of yellow and red.

2. I am very common in the countryside, but my origin is far away. I scratch the ground to unearth food. While I live on the ground, I usually spend the night up in a tree.

3. I am famous for running along beaches, dodging the waves and surf. Not many people know that I run so often that I have lost my hind toe. I have a very different colour in summer and winter.

4. For a long time I was extinct in Britain, but closing wetlands for war defences enabled me to recolonise in the 1940s. Since then, things have been on the up, especially my bill.

5. I am often ignored when people look for puffins on sea cliffs, but I make a very loud, wailing call so they always know I am there. I breed on precipitous cliffs, but also sometimes buildings. I am the most attractive member of my family, in many people's view.

6. I eat insects, which I catch in flight, and often live along rivers, burrowing a tunnel into the banks.

7. I am a member of the thrush family, and most people see me only in the winter, when I live in flocks and feed on the ground, or feast on berries. I am named for the colour of my flanks, but the easiest way to identify me is by a stripe over my eye.

8. I am well known for my habit of sitting upright on a perch, often a gorse bush. I also draw attention to myself by my persistent calling, and I also sing in flight. I am proud of my black tail.

9. I am famous, indirectly, for keeping many people warm and comfortable at night. I live by or in the sea, in colonies. In spring I can make suggestive crooning noises.

10. Anglers don't like me, especially on inland waters, because I am better at catching fish than they are. After another successful dive I hold out my wings to dry.

Did You Know?

In the nest, young kingfishers adopt
a circle and wait in turn to be fed,
shifting round after their turn.

General Knowledge

Seabirds

1. What unusual feeding technique do terns employ?

2. What is Britain's largest breeding seabird?

3. Why is the term 'seagull' frowned on by birdwatchers?

4. What highly effective defence do fulmars use when their nest is threatened?

5. How many eggs do gulls usually lay?

6. What is unusual about the shape of a guillemot's egg?

7. What colour is the blob near the tip of a herring gull's yellow bill, and how is it useful for chicks?

8. How does a young guillemot leave its cliff-ledge home when it has grown up?

9. How does a Manx shearwater find its nest hole when it returns, as it usually does, in the dark?

10. Why do Manx shearwaters and storm petrels tend to visit their burrows in the darkness?

Answers on page 225

PUZZLE 53

Fitword

Can you place all of these seabirds into the grid, crossword style?

Three-letter word
Auk

Four-letter words
Gull
Skua
Tern

Five-letter word
Eider

Six-letter words
Fulmar
Gannet
Petrel
Puffin

Nine-letter words
Cormorant
Kittiwake

Ten-letter word
Shearwater

Answers on page 226

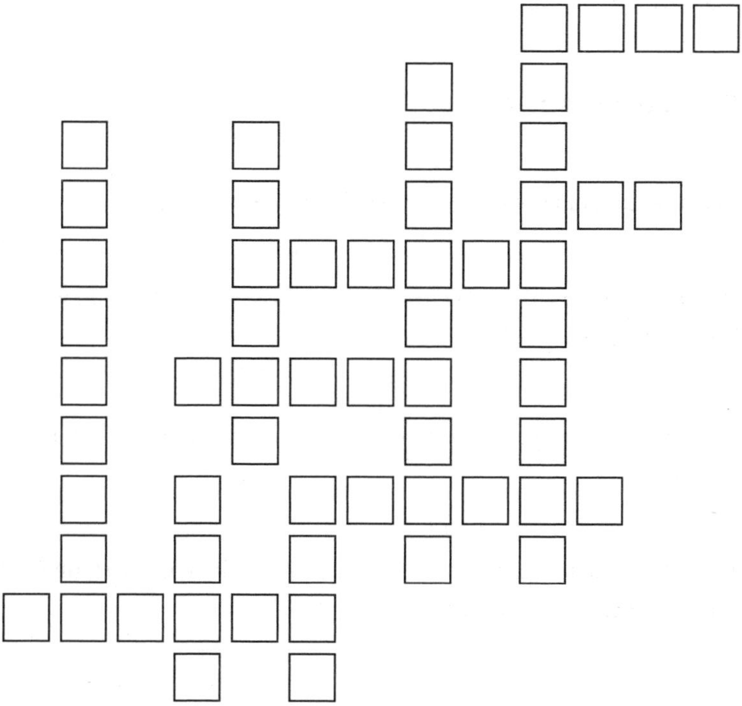

PUZZLE 54

Multiple Choice

1. What maximum nesting density can guillemot colonies acquire, in terms of nest sites per square metre?

    a. *21*　　　**b.** *76*

    c. *10*　　　**d.** *41*

2. How many times can a yellowhammer sing in a day?

    a. *500*　　　**b.** *1,000*

    c. *5,000*　　　**d.** *7,000*

3. What strange behavioural quirk does a redstart show?

    a. *It shivers its tail*　　　**b.** *It dangles its legs as it flies from the ground to a perch*

    c. *It sunbathes*　　　**d.** *It only sings from inside its nest hole*

4. What's the preferred food of the red grouse?

    a. *Seeds and leaves of the starry saxifrage*　　　**b.** *Small insects found on peat*

    c. *Heather shoots*　　　**d.** *Lichens and mosses in bogs*

5. What's the preferred habitat of the marsh tit?

    a. *Marshes*　　**b.** *Conifer woods*

    c. *Heaths*　　**d.** *Deciduous woods*

6. When did the first little egrets nest in Britain, on Brownsea Island?

    a. *1976*　　　**b.** *1986*

    c. *1996*　　　**d.** *2006*

7. The redstart, wood warbler and pied flycatcher are all typical of which distinctive habitat?

    a. *Alder woods*　　　**b.** *English (Pedunculate) oak woods*

    c. *Beech woods*　　　**d.** *Sessile oak woods*

8. The honey buzzard is a rare breeding bird in Britain. What is its main food during the summer?

    a. *Adult bees*　　　**b.** *Bee grubs*

    c. *Wasp grubs*　　　**d.** *Dragonflies*

9. What is the favourite food of the brent goose, a common wintering bird of the coasts of the British Isles?

    a. *Algae (seaweed)*　　　**b.** *Eelgrass*

    c. *Shrimps*　　　**d.** *Curry*

10. Where would you find a purple sandpiper in the winter in Britain?

    a. *Rocky coasts and jetties*　　　**b.** *Muddy estuaries*

    c. *Ditches in freshwater*　　　**d.** *Among heather*

Answers on page 226

PUZZLE 55

Mix and Match

Can you tally the bird to its habitat?

CETTI'S WARBLER   Wetlands and bogs

RED-THROATED DIVER   Fast-flowing streams

DARTFORD WARBLER   Lowland heathland

PTARMIGAN   Marshes and reed beds

CHOUGH •   Small Scottish lochs and sea
                                   coast

WHEATEAR   High, bleak mountain
                                   plateaux

GOSHAWK   Rocky and stony places,
                                   especially uplands

DIPPER   Large forests and nearby open
                                   areas

COMMON SNIPE

WATER RAIL   • Coastal cliffs, crags

                                   Reed beds and wetlands

Answers on page 226

PUZZLE 56

Crossword

Across

2. Season just before migrating birds head south for warmer climes (6)

7. Land along the edge of 14 across (5)

8. Land area near 14 across, generically (5)

9. Fish related to 25 across, eaten by gannets (5)

10. Game bird found on heathery uplands (6)

12. Nocturnal bird of prey (3)

14. Large expanse of salty water (3)

17. Bird of prey of the family *Accipitridae* (4)

18. Northumberland island group with large seabird colonies (5)

20. Steep rock face where seabirds might nest (5)

21. Come to a place temporarily, as a migrating bird might (5)

24. Relating to 14 across (6)

25. Plentiful fish which gives its name to a species of 10 down (7)

Down

1. Structure for birds to lay eggs and feed their young (4)

3. Small mammal eaten by owls and kites (5)

4. Smallest species of tern (6)

5. Crustacean eaten by sanderlings (4)

6. Open, uncultivated land where 10 across can be found (4)

10. Common seabird with a noisy cry (4)

11. Northern European peninsula from which waxwings migrate (11)

13. Large body of fresh water where moorhens may breed (4)

15. Chick of *Fratercula arctica* (8)

16. Long-tailed game bird with brilliant feathers (8)

19. Flowing body of water where goosanders might be found (5)

22. Repetitive rise and fall of the sea (4)

23. Hunted quarry (4)

Answers on page 227

Mix and Match

Can you tally the bird to its physical feature?

STONE-CURLEW •   White chin (as if it's cut itself
                                        shaving)

CANADA GOOSE
                                        Lyre-shaped tail in male

SAND MARTIN
                                        • Staring yellow eye

BLACK GUILLEMOT
                                        Black-and-white (zebra crossing)
                                        mark on neck
NIGHTJAR

                                        Tiny bill conceals huge mouth
TURTLE DOVE

                                        Kingfisher-blue patch on wing
NUTHATCH

                                        Brown band across chest
JAY

                                        Black stripe through eye
SISKIN

                                        Yellow wing-bars
BLACK GROUSE

                                        Bright red legs and feet

General Knowledge

Colours

How closely have you looked at your coastal and countryside birds recently? See if you can remember some of their colours.

1. What colour are the legs of a common whitethroat?

2. What colour is the rump (lower back, above the tail) of a yellowhammer?

3. What colour is a tufted duck's eye?

4. What colour are the feet of a little egret?

5. What colour are the scapulars (shoulders) of a brambling?

6. What colour are the legs of a puffin?

7. What colour are the underparts (chest, breast, belly) of a grey wagtail?

8. What colour are an avocet's legs?

9. What colour is a treecreeper underneath?

10. What colour is the tail of a fieldfare?

Answers on page 228

Mix and Match

Special Places

There are certain places in our islands that have a strong connection with some of our birds. See if you can match the bird to its special place.

AVOCET	Havergate Island, Suffolk
DARTFORD WARBLER	The Isle of Mull
PUFFIN	Lizard Point, Cornwall
MANX SHEARWATER	Devon coast
CHOUGH	Loch Garten, Highland
CIRL BUNTING	Skomer Island, Wales
ARCTIC AND SANDWICH TERN	Farne Islands, Northumberland
WHITE-TAILED EAGLE	Somerset Levels
STARLING (OR GREAT EGRET)	Isle of Man
OSPREY	Dartford Heath, London

Word Ladder

Complete each of these word ladders by writing a regular English word at each step. Each word must use the exact same letters in the same order as the word above, except with a single letter changed.

For example:

SHOW > SHOT > SOOT > SORT > SORE > MORE

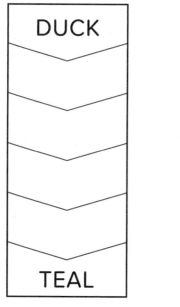

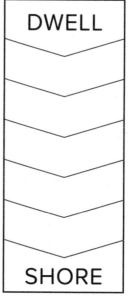

Multiple Choice
Waders (Shorebirds)

1. Which is Britain's largest wader?

   a. *Curlew* **b.** *Turnstone*

   c. *Bar-tailed godwit* **d.** *Redshank*

2. What is unusual about where a green sandpiper nests?

   a. *It nests behind a waterfall* **b.** *It nests in old nests above ground*

   c. *It nests near the den of a polar bear* **d.** *It nests on top of a hill*

3. What is the unusual name, derived from Swedish, for a gathering of male ruffs that display together?

   a. *Lick* **b.** *Lock*

   c. *Lurk* **d.** *Lek*

4. What unusual form of behaviour is often a great clue to telling a jack snipe from a common snipe?

   a. *It bobs up and down* **b.** *It points its bill upwards*

   c. *Frequent swimming* **d.** *It flaps its wings together to make noise*

5. What is the name of the RSPB reserve on The Wash, in East Anglia, famous for its enormous winter flocks and roosts of knots and other waders?

   a. *Snettisham* **b.** *Minsmere*

   c. *Titchwell* **d.** *Titchfield*

6. What's unusual about the relationship between the sexes in the dotterel (and also phalaropes)?

   a. *They largely ignore each other*

   b. *Male and female reverse roles with male looking after eggs and young*

   c. *The sexes only meet for a few moments to mate*

   d. *The male migrates south as soon as it has mated*

7. With a few exceptions, how many eggs constitute the clutch of most waders?

    a. *Seven*   **b.** *Six*

    c. *Four*   **d.** *Two*

8. What's unusual about the sounds made in display by the common snipe in flight?

    a. *It is made by their open bill*   **b.** *It is made by their feet*

    c. *It is made by females only*   **d.** *It is made by their tail feathers*

9. What is the woodcock's favourite food?

    a. *Worms*   **b.** *Dung*

    c. *Flies*   **d.** *Pizza*

10. What is the unusual feeding technique regularly used by the turnstone?

    a. *It hammers shells with its powerful bill*   **b.** *It turns things over*

    c. *It swims in the water*   **d.** *It probes deep into the mud*

Did You Know?

Scientists have now discovered that individual birds
have personalities. Some take more risks and are
more prone to explore new things and places.
Let's hope no seabirds breeding in huge
colonies are introverts!

Answers on page 229

Odd One Out
Bird Sightings

The following lists from birdwatching trips all contain a dodgy entry, with a bird that doesn't fit. Can you spot which one is wrong? These are particularly tricky, so there are clues below if you need a little help.

1. Cairngorms, March 2022

a. *Ptarmigan*   **b.** *Snow bunting*   **c.** *Cirl bunting*
d. *Common crossbill*   **e.** *Hooded crow*

2. Hampshire, April 2021

a. *Pheasant*   **b.** *Willow warbler*   **c.** *Red kite*
d. *Black grouse*   **e.** *Great tit*

3. Hampshire, April 1901

a. *Pheasant*   **b.** *Willow warbler*   **c.** *Red kite*
d. *Black grouse*   **e.** *Great tit*

4. Isles of Scilly, May 2019

a. *Manx shearwater*   **b.** *Song thrush*   **c.** *Puffin*
d. *Blackbird*   **e.** *Long-tailed tit*

5. Garden in London, December 2020

a. *Woodpigeon*   **b.** *Robin*   **c.** *Nightingale*
d. *Blue tit*   **e.** *Magpie*

6. Hertfordshire, April 1920

a. *Feral pigeon*   **b.** *Woodpigeon*   **c.** *Stock dove*
d. *Collared dove*   **e.** *Turtle dove*

7. North Yorkshire, November 2021

a. *Raven*   **b.** *Red grouse*   **c.** *Yellow grouse*

d. *Yellowhammer*   **e.** *Merlin*

8. Garden in Manchester, January 1999

a. *Blue tit*   **b.** *Great tit*   **c.** *Blackbird*

d. *Woodpigeon*   **e.** *Puffin*

9. White Cliffs of Dover, April 2022

a. *Eastern bluebird*   **b.** *Cormorant*   **c.** *Swallow*

d. *Stock dove*   **e.** *Linnet*

10. Reedbed at RSPB Lakenheath, Suffolk, June 2015

a. *Bittern*   **b.** *Water rail*   **c.** *Reed warbler*

d. *Reed bunting*   **e.** *Wood warbler*

Clues:

1. This bird is only found on the south coast of England.
2. This bird is now extinct in Hampshire.
3. This bird was only later reintroduced in Hampshire, but at this time was extinct.
4. This bird doesn't occur here.
5. This bird has migrated away.
6. This bird didn't appear in Britain until the mid-1950s.
7. This bird doesn't exist.
8. This bird should be out at sea.
9. This bird has never been recorded in Britain.
10. This is a woodland bird.

Did You Know?

The northern wheatear breeds everywhere between the Arctic and the Mediterranean, and anywhere from sea level up to 2,500m (8,200ft) in altitude.

Hidden Names

Can you work out the name of the bird missing from the sentence
or phrase? This quiz is a bit corny!

1. Sadly, things remain a _ _ _ _ _ _ _ _ _ -ward between us.

2. Get up. Don't just _ _ _ _ _ _ _ _ -bout the bush.

3. She is gambling everything on this. She's a real high _ _ _ _ _ _.

4. It's three _ _ _ _ _ _ _ and you're out.

5. We're getting short of _ _ _ _ _ _ ,we need to fill up.

6. It's important in life to know your _ _ _ _ _ _ _.

7. There are 24 _ _ _ _ _ _ _ _ _ _ making up a foot.

8. R_ _ _ _ _ _ , I've had a few.

9. It's been so cold that my fingers are frost _ _ _ _ _ _ _.

10. I will definitely accept that. I think you got it about _ _ _ _ _.

PUZZLE 64

Word Circle

Rearrange the letters in the circle below to reveal a seabird which lays its eggs on bare rock. Then, how many other words can you find that use the centre letter plus two or more of the other letters? No letter may be used more times than it appears within the circle.

General Knowledge
Birds of Prey and Owls

1. Which bird of prey famously dives into the water to catch fish?

2. What is the main diet of the red kite?

3. What bird of prey is most likely to leave a pile of feathers on your lawn after an attack on the bird feeders?

4. Which bird of prey is so fast and agile that it can catch a swift in flight?

5. Which is Britain's noisiest raptor, which makes mewing calls to defend its territory over woods and fields?

6. What is the main difference in prey preference between a kestrel and a sparrowhawk?

7. What raptor is famously the subject of controversy between conservationists and the owners of grouse-shooting estates?

8. Which owl famously hoots 'tu-whit, tu-whoo', but equally famously, doesn't.

9. What is the only British owl that actually screeches?

10. What mammal often features high on the menu of the golden eagle in the Highlands of Scotland?

Answers on page 230

CHAPTER FOUR

BIRD BIOLOGY

Parts of a Bird

Can you assign the technical name to the part of the bird
indicated on the diagram?

FLANKS

CROWN

RUMP

NAPE

MANTLE

THROAT

SUPERCILIUM

CULMEN (UPPER MANDIBLE)

LORES

COVERTS

PUZZLE 67

Word Circle

Rearrange the letters in the circle below to reveal a scientific profession for which Carl Linnaeus is well known. Then, how many other words can you find that use the centre letter plus two or more of the other letters? No letter may be used more times than it appears within the circle.

Mix and Match

Scientific Names

The scientific names of birds are not well known, but some are descriptive and others are evocative. See if you can match the bird to its scientific name.

TURTLE DOVE	*Puffinus puffinus*
WATER RAIL	*Troglodytes troglodytes*
MANX SHEARWATER	*Recurvirostra avosetta*
KNOT	*Cettia cetti*
WREN	*Passer domesticus*
MAGPIE	*Falco subbuteo*
AVOCET	*Rallus aquaticus*
HOUSE SPARROW	*Calidris canutus*
CETTI'S WARBLER	*Streptopelia turtur*
HOBBY	*Pica pica*

PUZZLE 69

True or False?

	True	False
1. Owls can turn their heads up to 360 degrees.		
2. The plumage of some birds will change between summer and winter.		
3. Most birds have hollow bones.		
4. An owl has three eyelids.		
5. Gannets have flaps over their nostrils so that when they dive into the water, it doesn't go up their nose and damage their brain.		
6. Feathers are made up mainly from keratin, a similar substance to that making up our fingernails.		
7. Despite their different sizes, all birds have approximately the same number of feathers.		
8. A bird's organs, from the gut to the gonads, may be completely different sizes at different times of year.		
9. A bird with a vegetarian diet has a shorter gut than a meat eater, because their food is easier to digest.		
10. Seabirds can drink salt water without killing themselves.		

Answers on page 232

Codeword

Solve the following codeword and then rearrange the shaded squares to reveal a verb related to taxonomies. A codeword is a coded crossword in which every letter has been replaced by a number, indicated by the small digits in the top left corner of each crossword square.

As a further clue, the puzzle also contains four features that can be used in identifying birds. Other words, however, are not bird-related.

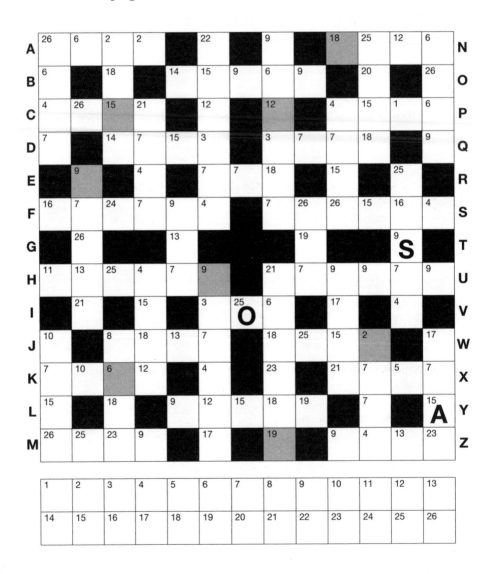

General Knowledge

Plumage

1. Which British bird has feathered feet?

2. What is the main moulting season for birds?

3. Why do birds often look fat in the winter?

4. The feather is shaped rather like a trunk with branches. What is the 'trunk' (the central bough of the feather) called?

5. And what are the 'branches' called coming off the main stalk of the feather?

6. What irritating pests often live on the feathers of living birds?

7. Which colours seen on feathers are not pigments, but reflected light?

8. What is the term for the shiny, glittering effect of this light?

9. What is eclipse plumage?

10. Why do birds need to moult their feathers?

Multiple Choice

Senses

1. Barn owls can catch prey in complete darkness, using only their hearing. What curious adaptation is thought to enable them to do this?

   a. *They have three ears*

   b. *One ear is higher up on the skull than the other*

   c. *They nod their head very fast when sensing prey*

   d. *The two ears have different sensitivities*

2. Tawny owls have better hearing than people but by how much, approximately?

   a. *× 10* **b.** *× 6.2*

   c. *× 2.2* **d.** *× 3.8*

3. Which British bird has its eyes placed so completely on the side of its head that it has complete 360 degree vision, and has overlapping vision front and back?

   a. *Robin* **b.** *Mute swan*

   c. *Woodcock* **d.** *Pheasant*

4. In recent experiments it has been shown that pigeons can hear sounds far deeper than those detectable to humans. What are these sounds called?

   a. *Infrasounds* **b.** *Ultrasounds*

   c. *Deep sounds* **d.** *Thunder sounds*

5. Birds are famous for having a magnetic sense, which helps them orientate during migration but how do they detect the Earth's magnetic field?

   a. *With the ears* **b.** *Vibrations in the tongue*

   c. *Through the eyes* **d.** *Receptors on the bill*

6. Waders often have vast numbers of receptors at the tip of their bill, known as Herbst's corpuscles. What do they sense?

   a. *Odour* **b.** *Touch*

   c. *Electromagnetic fields* **d.** *Taste*

7. What do starlings use their sense of smell to do?

   a. *Find food in the grass*

   b. *Select a mate*

   c. *Find flock-mates with which to roost*

   d. *Find specific plants for the nest*

8. Which of these birds finds a substantial proportion of its food using smell?

   a. *Razorbill*   **b.** *Storm petrel*

   c. *Gannet*   **d.** *Cormorant*

9. It is thought that migratory thrushes have a special way of detecting berries. How do they find them?

   a. *They can detect ultraviolet from the berries*

   b. *They can smell berries from a distance*

   c. *Berries growing on bushes give off high-pitched sound*

   d. *Berries give off a magnetic signal*

10. Recent examinations on taste buds in mallard ducks showed that:

    a. *They have no taste buds*

    b. *They do have taste buds that are all on the tongue*

    c. *They do have taste buds but are only on the bill tip*

    d. *They do have taste buds that are on the tongue, bill tip and floor of the mouth*

Did You Know?

A study of grey herons in Yorkshire found that for 77 per cent of the day they do nothing! They just stand still, awake but inactive.

Pathfinder

Can you find seven species of goose in the grid below? Starting at the shaded square, find a path that visits every grid square exactly once each, spelling out the species' names as it goes. The path can only travel horizontally or vertically between squares, and should end at the star.

Some of the geese species have two words, while others have one. In addition, the letters at the following steps in your path will spell out, in order, the name of a final goose: first, third, eighth, eleventh and fifteenth. What is that goose?

	N	A	D	A	T	A	N
B	A	C	E	I	A	E	W
A	R	N	L	G	A	B	H
D	E	A	C	F	E	T	I
G	T	N	O	R	T	U	N
R	G	P	T	E	D	R	D
E	A	I	O	O	B	A	☆
Y	L	N	K	F	E	A	N

PUZZLE 74

Finding Your Feet

Can you identify the birds from their feet?

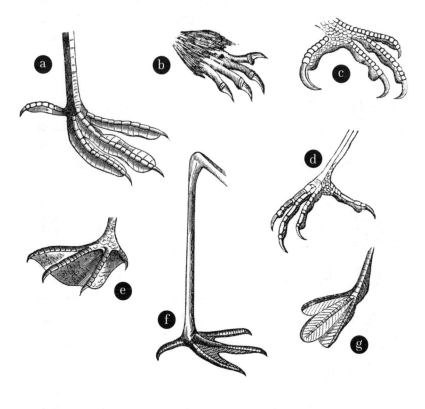

a _____

b _____

c _____

d _____

e _____

f _____

g _____

Sparrow	Swift	Heron	Duck
Eagle	Coot	Grebe	

True or False?

Fossil Birds

	True	False
1. Birds are the only living dinosaurs.		
2. Birds have always been distinguished from reptiles and mammals because they have no teeth.		
3. Birds are close relatives of their colleagues in the air, the pterosaurs.		
4. Many early birds were much larger than those seen today.		
5. There is good early evidence that, many years ago, some birds caught and ate live humans.		
6. Hummingbirds are among the few families of birds for which we have no fossils.		
7. The first known bird is *Archaeopteryx*, which lived about 150 million years ago.		
8. A wonderful range of bird fossils has been found recently in Russia, adding enormously to our knowledge of how birds evolved.		
9. Whenever lists of birds of the world are created, they begin with the most ancient birds and finish with those that evolved most recently.		
10. We know considerably more about Tyrannosaurus rex, extinct 66 million years ago, than we do about the dodo, extinct 1689.		

Answers on page 234

PUZZLE 76

Mix and Match

Families and Relatives

Here are two lists of ten birds. Your task is to pair the two species
that are in the same family.

SAND MARTIN	JACKDAW
GREY WAGTAIL	BULLFINCH
JAY	SPOONBILL
GLOSSY IBIS	MALLARD
EIDER	MEADOW PIPIT
REDPOLL	SWALLOW
RED KITE	WHITE-TAILED EAGLE
BLACKCAP	MERLIN
DUNLIN	BAR-TAILED GODWIT
KESTREL	DARTFORD WARBLER

Word Ladder

Complete each of these word ladders by writing a regular English word at each step. Each word must use the exact same letters in the same order as the word above, except with a single letter changed.

For example:

SHOW > SHOT > SOOT > SORT > SORE > MORE

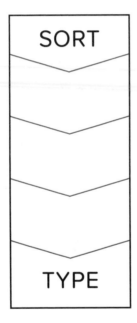

SORT

TYPE

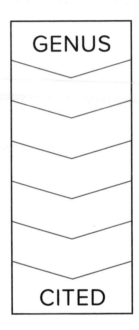

GENUS

CITED

General Knowledge
Bills

1. What diet are birds with short, thick, cone-shaped beaks likely to have?

2. What diet is a straight, thin beak adapted towards?

3. How do birds grind up their food?

4. What advantages does a long, curved bill confer?

5. Which British bird has the longest bill relative to its size?

6. How can you tell a female curlew's bill from that of a male?

7. What is the difference between a beak and a bill?

8. What aspect of the bill enables you to tell a male from a female kingfisher?

9. What unusual bill adaptation do goosanders, red-breasted mergansers and smews have?

10. What unusual feature, other than size, does the bill of a shoveler have?

Multiple Choice

Flight

How much do you know about bird flight? Here are ten multiple choice questions to test you.

1. What term is used for circling upwards, often seen in birds of prey and seabirds?

   a. *Soaring* **b.** *Gliding*
   c. *Hovering* **d.** *Banking*

2. What term is used for moving forwards without flapping the wings?

   a. *Soaring* **b.** *Gliding*
   c. *Hovering* **d.** *Careening*

3. Most small birds fly with a distinctive up and down flight, known as 'undulating' or 'bounding'. Which of these species doesn't do it?

   a. *Great tit* **b.** *Chaffinch*
   c. *Little owl* **d.** *Bearded tit*

4. What term is used for rapidly flapping the wings to keep the body in one place, as seen in kestrels, kingfishers and terns?

   a. *Soaring* **b.** *Gliding*
   c. *Hovering* **d.** *Quartering*

5. How fast can an eider fly?

   a. *223 km/h (139 mph)*
   b. *95 km/h (59 mph)*
   c. *170 km/h (106 mph)*
   d. *123 km/h (76 mph)*

6. What term is used for a very slow and low flight over the ground, described as similar to 'looking for a lost golf ball', used by harriers and short-eared owls?

   a. *Quartering* **b.** *Halving*
   c. *Churning* **d.** *Propping*

7. Many species fly in a particular formation to save energy. What letter represents the ideal shape?

   a. *V* **b.** *U*
   c. *I* **d.** *C*

8. What wing shape is best for fast, agile flight?

   a. *Long, rounded wings*
   b. *Short, rounded wings*
   c. *Long, pointed wings*
   d. *Short, pointed wings*

9. What is a swift's maximum speed?

   a. *53 km/h (33 mph)*
   b. *166 km/h (103 mph)*
   c. *230 km/h (143 mph)*
   d. *300 km/h (186 mph)*

10. Which is arguably Britain's most reluctant flying bird, spending more time on the ground than any other?

    a. *Red grouse* **b.** *Blackbird*
    c. *Grey partridge* **d.** *Water rail*

PUZZLE 80

True or False?

	True	False
1. Pigeons and doves are the only British birds that can suck up water.		
2. The keel bone (wishbone) is unique to birds.		
3. Birds urinate as well as defaecate, but it is rarely observed.		
4. Birds have a breathing system identical to ours.		
5. Birds are warm-blooded.		
6. Some birds, such as storks, poo on their legs to keep them cool.		
7. The bones of a bird are hollow and contain many air sacs.		
8. Birds have many sweat-glands under the feathers.		
9. In some cases, a bird's sound production system (the syrinx) allows it to sing two songs at the same time.		
10. The large intestine is the longest part of a bird's digestive system.		

Answers on page 236

PUZZLE 81

Crossword

Across

4. Taxonomic rank (5)

6. Famous proponent of the theory of evolution (6)

7. Innate, unconscious behaviour, such as homing (8)

8. Large animal community, as seabirds might form (6)

11. An animal's defended domain (9)

14. Protected area for birds and other wildlife (7)

16. Taxonomic rank (5)

17. Arrange into categories according to similarities (8)

18. Type of bird studied closely by 6 across (5)

19. Lose feathers before new growth (5)

20. Be in a dormant state for the winter (9)

Down

1. Bird or animal which gives clues about general habitat change (9)

2. The study of birds (11)

3. Any bird of prey, such as a hawk (6)

5. Arrangement of wildlife over a large area (12)

9. Produce, as 15 down (3)

10. Botanist, zoologist or oologist (10)

12. Juvenile (5)

13. Large order of birds, which includes songbirds (9)

15. Something deceptively planted by cuckoos (3)

Hidden Names

Can you find the names of the birds hidden in these sentences?

1. Remarkably, offal continues to be eaten in the UK, mostly as black pudding.

2. Back in the 11th century, King Cnut hatched a clever plan to show his humility to his English subjects by failing to hold back the tide.

3. Walking down by the riverside, I was delighted to see some flowering water avens (*Geum rivale*).

4. They all flew north, rushing to be the first on territory.

5. I hadn't realised that the party was over and was embarrassed to be the last one chatting.

6. The car's chassis kind of buckled below us, which was disconcerting.

7. Look at the gorgeous detail on those beautiful, scarred, pollarded willows.

8. We enjoyed a long session looking up at the stars, despite the bitter night.

9. Both John Stones and Erling Haaland are brilliant players for Manchester City.

10. Little George is enjoying his gift of Duplo very much.

Wordsearch

Genus Species

All of the words in this wordsearch can be doubled to form both the genus and species of a bird. For example, *Alle alle* is the little auk. Find them all in the grid – although just a single time each.

```
C O D R I R A U R E G U L U S
S U L L E N A V M L I M O S A
S I R O L H C N N P E R D I X
P O P X I N R U T O C R R T L
S G E S E R I N U S L A R A U
S U S T P A S I T L P O C R M
U U U U U I A Y G I G I S I C
L C N E L B N A R L P S L I A
R Y U I U O L U O V C V C L G
U G A U F L I D S V U O L C R
Y N G P I F Y R G S N E P Y U
S U C N U T U V O I R I Y N S
S S A O E S M P A S C R E X P
N G U S N X A R O C I T C Y N
O T A D O R N A M R R G G S S
```

ALLE	GALLINAGO	PUFFINUS
APUS	GRUS	REGULUS
BUTEO	LIMOSA	RIPARIA
CHLORIS	MILVUS	SERINUS
CICONIA	NYCTICORAX	SPINUS
COTURNIX	ORIOLUS	TADORNA
CREX	PERDIX	TROGLODYTES
CYGNUS	PICA	VANELLUS

What Bird Am I?

Two birdwatchers have just seen a bird that they didn't recognise. They watched it carefully and noted quite a few features – this is an extract from their notebook. What do you think they saw?

We saw a strange bird running in a field.

It didn't run all the time, though. It would run along and then suddenly stop, then run off in a different direction.

When it flew off it looked completely different, quite big with rounded wings.

It had iridescent, metallic colours on the back.

The bill was short and straight.

The head was adorned with a strange, wispy crest, which was easily ruffled like a lock of hair.

It had a curious, insistent whining call.

It seemed to be eating something from the ground, something like worms.

When we looked later, there were others with it, making a flock.

When flying, it didn't seem very powerful, like ash blowing in the wind.

Fitword

Can you place all these parts of a bird into the grid, crossword style?

Three-letter word
Toe

Four-letter words
Back
Band
Bill
Chin
Claw
Edge
Nape
Rump
Tail
Vent

Five-letter words
Alula
Belly
Brace
Crown
Flank
Tibia

Six-letter words
Breast
Mantle
Tarsus
Throat

Seven-letter words
Coverts
Primary
Tertial

Eight-letter words
Forehead
Hindneck
Mandible
Scapular

Nine-letter word
Secondary

What Bird Am I?

Can you work out the species from the following statements about its anatomy and lifestyle?

My second and third toes are partly joined together on my small feet.

My bill is long, straight and laterally flattened.

I spend much time perching and looking down.

My eyes are specially adapted so that, when I do look down, I have a very good judge of distance.

I don't like being disturbed, so I'm very aggressive if someone invades my territory.

I catch food by plunging into the water.

When I am feeding, I have to compensate for refraction, making things below the water surface look closer than they are.

In the breeding season I use my bill to dig.

My plumage is brilliantly coloured.

I fly very low down and rapidly, with fast wing-beats.

Did You Know?

Of all British birds, the jackdaw is the most faithful to its partner – not the swan. Only one per cent of jackdaw chicks are reared by a bird that isn't the genetic parent.

CHAPTER FIVE

A HISTORY OF BIRDS

Crossword

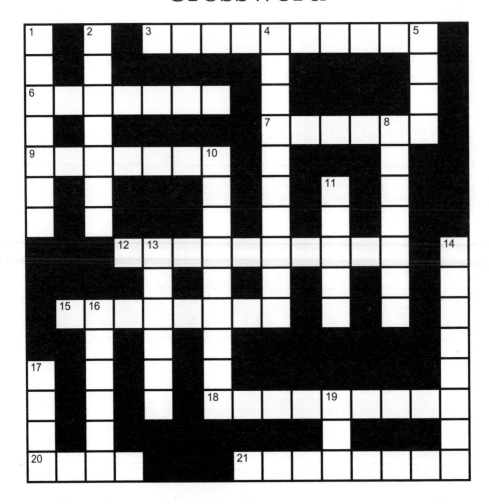

Across

3. Bird known for its rhythmic tapping, increasingly seen in gardens (10)

6. Noticed; bearing a speckled pattern (7)

7. Possessing a feathery crest (6)

9. Small songbird family; festive flag garland (7)

12. Commonly seen bird related to the dove (10)

15. Organised movement pressing for action (8)

18. Suffolk island and nature reserve (9)

20. Toy flown in the wind; bird of prey (4)

21. Native, untamed fauna (8)

Down

1. Human-made place for a bird to rear chicks (4, 3)

2. Legendary reincarnating bird (7)

4. Guardianship; safekeeping (10)

5. Grass-like plant; species of warbler (4)

8. No longer living, as a species (7)

10. Seed-eating bird with yellow plumage (9)

11. Large; largest tit family member (5)

13. Large, fish-eating bird of prey (6)

14. RSPB nature reserve in Suffolk (8)

16. Bird appearing on the RSPB logo (6)

17. Drop down to avoid; common waterbird (4)

19. Primary colour; prospering species of 20 across (3)

Answers on page 239

Mix and Match

Breeding Pairs

Can you match the bird to the number of breeding pairs in Britain? Write them in order from the most abundant to the least abundant.

In the correct order, the first letters of each bird spell out another name, which matches the extra number.

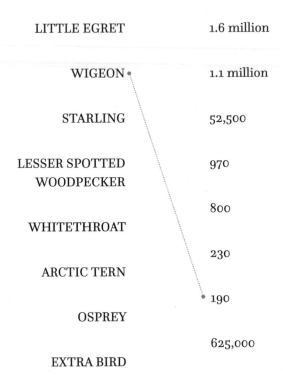

LITTLE EGRET	1.6 million
WIGEON	1.1 million
STARLING	52,500
LESSER SPOTTED WOODPECKER	970
	800
WHITETHROAT	
	230
ARCTIC TERN	
	190
OSPREY	
	625,000
EXTRA BIRD	

Figures are taken from *RSPB Handbook of British Birds* (Bloomsbury; Fifth Edition, 2021).

General Knowledge

Introduced Species

How well do you know the birds that aren't native to Britain, but have been introduced? Try out these general knowledge questions.

1. In what century was the Canada goose first introduced to Britain?

2. Which of our owls was introduced in the mid 1800s?

3. Name one of the two rare ornamental pheasants that have been introduced to Britain (not the common pheasant).

4. Which ornamental duck is prospering and expanding its range here in Britain, but declining in its native breeding range in Asia?

5. Roughly where might you find the closest (to UK) truly wild representatives of the pheasant?

6. Which bird is currently being introduced to Britain (in Sussex), having previously only bred here in 1416 (as of 2022)?

7. Which magnificent, previously native species is currently being reintroduced to Salisbury Plain (as of 2022)?

8. Red kites are now seen in many places in Britain, but where was the last bastion for wild red kites before the conservation efforts began?

9. Which duck, introduced by accident in the 1950s, prospered until it was controversially culled from 2005–10?

10. From where does our non-native partridge, the red-legged partridge, originate?

Answers on page 240

Multiple Choice

Britain has some of the best documented bird populations in the world, and not surprisingly, a lot of facts and figures. See how well you know the fortunes of some of our birds.

1. What is the most numerous bird in the UK?

   a. *Wren*   **b.** *Chaffinch*

   c. *Woodpigeon*   **d.** *Blue tit*

2. House sparrows are estimated to have declined in numbers by what percentage since 1977 (as of 2022)?

   a. *96 per cent*   **b.** *35 per cent*

   c. *71 per cent*   **d.** *58 per cent*

3. Which of these species has the highest population in Britain?

   a. *Grey heron*   **b.** *Herring gull*

   c. *Tufted duck*   **d.** *Canada goose*

4. In what year did the campaign to reintroduce the red kite to many of its former haunts begin?

   a. *1989*   **b.** *2001*

   c. *2010*   **d.** *1995*

5. Which species is Britain's fastest declining bird, now said by the Wildlife Trusts to be on the 'brink of extinction'?

   a. *Nightingale*   **b.** *Turtle dove*

   c. *Skylark*   **d.** *Greenfinch*

6. And by how much has it declined in breeding population between 1995 and 2018?

   a. *76 per cent*   **b.** *83 per cent*

   c. *95 per cent*   **d.** *90 per cent*

7. In 2010, the journalist Michael McCarthy published a book bemoaning the decline of a noisy spring bird. Its title was 'Say Goodbye to the .....'

   a. *Lesser black-backed gull*   **b.** *Cuckoo*

   c. *Nightingale*   **d.** *Song thrush*

8. Which species increased its population by 850 per cent between 1967 and 2017 and thus is Britain's fastest-increasing accurately measured bird?

   a. *Buzzard*   **b.** *Raven*

   c. *Cetti's warbler* **d.** *Magpie*

9. To measure bird fortunes, conservation organisations now have categories for those species of concern. What is the most serious category of list in terms of a bird's fortunes?

   a. *Amber List*   **b.** *Purple List*

   c. *Black List*   **d.** *Red List*

10. Which declining species is the subject of a bitter war between environmentalists and the owners of grouse-shooting estates?

    a. *Marsh harrier*   **b.** *Golden eagle*

    c. *Montagu's harrier* **d.** *Hen harrier*

Answers on page 240

PUZZLE 91

Wordsearch

In Decline

Can you find all of these birds that are 'threatened', or whose numbers are in decline (as of 2022), within the wordsearch grid? The names can read horizontally, vertically or diagonally, forwards or backwards.

```
T W O R R A P S E E R T L E W
L L U G G N I R R E H I E G P
I S K Y L A R K T A A I G D T
T S E Y I A N I R T L R N I S
T H T T M A T C G L T T I R R
L A H L H H T A I I U I T T E
E G U S S I W A P R G T N R L
T F D R C W C I T N N W U A B
E E A S O R P L I I I O B P R
R M K L E E E L L S W L N Y A
N U L P E D R N N A P L R E W
A E A R O A U I P R A I O R D
Y C T V T D P H C O L W C G O
P L E S S E R R E D P O L L O
V E L A G N I T H G I N A A W
```

ARCTIC SKUA
CAPERCAILLIE
CORN BUNTING
DUNLIN
FULMAR
GREY PARTRIDGE
HERRING GULL
LAPWING

LESSER REDPOLL
LITTLE TERN
MARSH TIT
NIGHTINGALE
REDSHANK
SHAG
SKYLARK
SNIPE

STARLING
TREE PIPIT
TREE SPARROW
TURTLE DOVE
WILLOW TIT
WOOD WARBLER
YELLOW WAGTAIL

PUZZLE 92

Codeword

Solve the following codeword and then rearrange the shaded squares to reveal a bird with a distinctive ascending two-note call. A codeword is a coded crossword in which every letter has been replaced by a number, indicated by the small digits in the top left corner of each crossword square.

As a further clue, the puzzle also contains two words that will surely be relevant to all those reading this book.

Pathfinder

Can you find 13 tasks carried out by conservationists in the grid below? Starting at the shaded square, find a path that visits every grid square exactly once each, spelling them out as it goes. The path can only travel horizontally or vertically between squares. As a clue, the tasks can be found in alphabetical order along the path.

A	S	S	E	S	A	T	E	G
C	T	H	C	S	M	G	U	A
O	R	A	S	T	I	E	I	N
U	C	T	E	T	I	M	M	F
N	E	T	R	O	N	O	R	O
T	D	E	R	U	R	V	E	Y
R	O	C	E	S	E	L	O	V
D	V	I	S	A	L	U	E	E
R	E	E	W	M	P	N	T	R

Word Ladder

Complete each of these word ladders by writing a regular English word at each step. Each word must use the exact same letters in the same order as the word above, except with a single letter changed.

For example:

SHOW > SHOT > SOOT > SORT > SORE > MORE

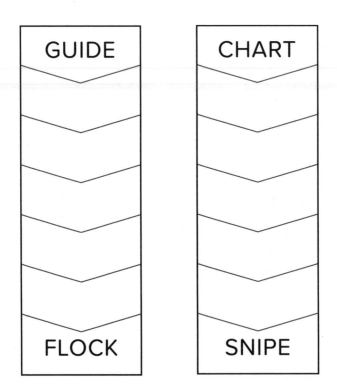

GUIDE

FLOCK

CHART

SNIPE

PUZZLE 95

Mix and Match

Folk Names

The UK has a rich history of local names for birds, many of which are delightful, some are quite rude and some are just weird. Can you match the folk name to the modern name of the bird?

BLACK GUILLEMOT	Throstle
GARDEN WARBLER	Bottle jug
LONG-TAILED TIT	Pettichaps
RINGED PLOVER	Bonxie
SONG THRUSH	Tystie
MISTLE THRUSH	Plover's page
GREAT SKUA	Scooper
GOLDFINCH	Storm cock
DUNLIN	Thistle warp
AVOCET	Dulwilly

PUZZLE 96

Word Circle

Rearrange the letters in the circle below to reveal a seabird whose numbers are in sharp decline. Then, how many other words can you find that use the centre letter plus two or more of the other letters? No letter may be used more times than it appears within the circle. These words also include three other birds.

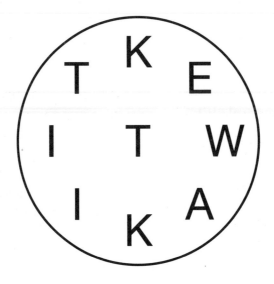

PUZZLE 97

Multiple Choice

Dates

The history of birds and people is long and textured. Can you work
out the dates of these events in the life of birds in the UK?

1. In what year was a live specimen of a dodo exhibited in London?

   a. *1638*   **b.** *1975*
   c. *1540*   **d.** *1800*

2. Until the current reintroduction, when was the last time a pair of white storks nested in Britain?

   a. *1416*   **b.** *1616*
   c. *1716*   **d.** *1916*

3. When did Emily Williamson first form the Society that would develop into the RSPB?

   a. *1901*   **b.** *1889*
   c. *1932*   **d.** *1850*

4. When did St Cerf of Culross keep a pet robin, the first known instance of its ease with human beings?

   a. *c.401*   **b.** *c.650*
   c. *c.580*   **d.** *1973*

5. When was the first standard 'field guide' published – *A Field Guide to the Birds of Britain and Europe*, by Peterson, Mountford and Hollom? Many others of similar ilk have followed.

   a. *1900*   **b.** *1933*
   c. *1921*   **d.** *1959*

6. When did ospreys first successfully breed at Loch Garten, after years of effort by conservationists?

   a. *1945*   **b.** *1963*
   c. *1959*   **d.** *1970*

7. When did the RSPB's Big Garden Birdwatch begin?

   a. *2003*   **b.** *1979*
   c. *2010*   **d.** *1988*

8. Aviaries at Foxwarren Park, near Wisley in Surrey, housed the last pink-headed ducks ever known to exist. The bird is extinct. But when was it?

   a. *1939*   **b.** *1835*
   c. *1789*   **d.** *1900*

9. When did the BBC's *Springwatch* first start?

   a. *1988*   **b.** *2005*
   c. *1997*   **d.** *2010*

10. When was the robin first declared Britain's National Bird, as voted in *The Times* newspaper?

   a. *1940*   **b.** *1960*
   c. *1950*   **d.** *1970*

Fitword

Can you place all of these ornithological surnames into the grid, crossword style?

Three-letter word

Low

Four-letter words

Kear

Knox

Snow

Five-letter words

Aplin

Cramp

Elwes

Six-letter words

Chance

Clarke

Newton

Oldham

Ramsay

Seven-letter words

Croxall

Edwards

Kinnear

Lilford

Thomson

Wallace

Mix and Match

Gains and Losses

Can you put the following nine birds into the most relevant categories below? Some have been lost, some gained, and some have been here since records began.

Select from the following list and put them in one of three categories:

COLLARED DOVE   CRESTED TIT   GREAT EGRET

GREY PARTRIDGE   KENTISH PLOVER   RED-BACKED SHRIKE

WRYNECK   DARTFORD WARBLER   CETTI'S WARBLER

A Recent gain as breeding bird (in last 75 years)	B Recent loss as breeding bird	C Always here
....	....	....
....	....	....
....	....	....

Mix and Match

Collective Nouns

Hardly anyone uses most of them, and they are mostly entirely archaic, but quiz setters and crossword fanatics cannot leave them alone. Can you match the bird to its collective noun?

SKYLARK	An exaltation
GREYLAG GOOSE	A murmuration
SNIPE	A murder
CARRION CROW	A charm
GOLDFINCH	A cast
SPARROWHAWK	A parliament
GREAT SPOTTED WOODPECKER	An unkindness
	A wisp
STARLING	A skein
RAVEN	A descent
ROOK	

CHAPTER SIX

WHAT'S THAT BIRD?

PUZZLE 101

Mix and Match

Can you identify the birds from these pictures?

1. ....

2. ....

3. ....

4. ....

5. ....

6. ....

7. ....

8. ....

STARLING

WHINCHAT

TREE SPARROW

BEE-EATER

COMMON BUZZARD

CORN BUNTING

SWALLOW

WHITE STORK

Answers on page 245

What Bird Am I?

Male or Female

Can you name the species, and tell which of these
is the male and female?

	Female	Male
1.		
a		
b		
2.		
a		
b		
3.		
a		
b		
4.		
a		
b		

PUZZLE 103

Spot the Difference

Can you identify ten differences between these two pictures?

PUZZLE 104

What Bird Am I?

Can you identify the birds in the vintage illustrations?

a ....   f ....

b ....   g ....

c ....   h ....

d ....   i ....

e ....   j ....

Answers on page 245

PUZZLE 105

Spot the Difference

Can you identify ten differences between these two pictures?

Answers on page 268–9

Mix and Match

Juveniles

Can you unravel the anagrams and identify the species
of these juvenile birds?

1.

2.

3.

5.

6.

4.

7.

8.

TOWNY LAW

NIFFUP

HUCKSLED

GOPINEWOOD

AWKGOSH

INCLUDES WRAPPER

ENFORCER LEAPING

TILL TOWEL

PUZZLE 107

What Bird Am I?

Study these illustrations. Can you name each bird?

1. ....

2. ....

3. ....

4. ....

5. ....

6. ....

7. ....

8. ....

Mix and Match

Can you name each species of bird below – and for a bonus point, do you know what they all have in common?

1. ....

2. ....

3. ....

4. ....

5. ....

SKYLARK

BLUETHROAT

BLACKCAP

MISTLE THRUSH

MARSH WARBLER

They are all ....

PUZZLE 109

What Bird Am I?

Study these illustrations. Can you name each bird?

1. ....

2. ....

3. ....

4. ....

5. ....

6. ....

7. ....

8. ....

Answers on page 246

Spot the Difference

Can you identify ten differences between these two pictures?

Answers on page 270–1

What Bird Am I?

Study these illustrations. Can you name each bird?

1. ....

2. ....

3. ....

4. ....

5. ....

6. ....

7. ....

8. ....

9. ....

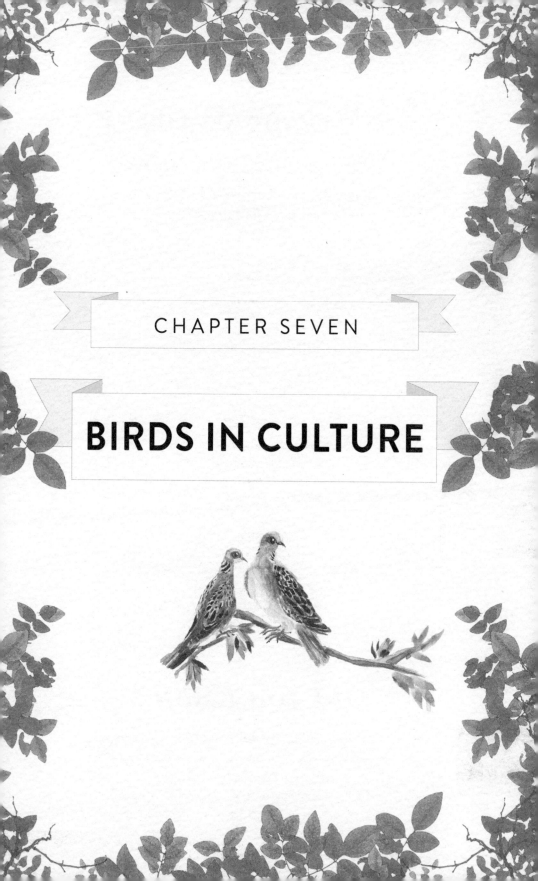

CHAPTER SEVEN

BIRDS IN CULTURE

Missing Words

Phrases and Expressions

Fill in the letters to reveal the bird in a
well-known expression.

1. Up with the ....

2. The .... that lays the golden egg.

3. As the .... flies.

4. Like a .... to water.

5. One .... doesn't make a summer.

6. A .... song.

7. Don't count your .... before they hatch.

8. Proud as a ....

9. An .... round the neck.

10. As bald as a ....

Did You Know?

The fieldfare is famous for pooing on its enemies.
If a predator attacks, one fieldfare after another
will dive-bomb and deliver!

PUZZLE 113

Fill in the Gap

Movie Titles

Complete the movie title with its missing bird.

1. One Flew Over the .... Nest

2. The Maltese ....

3. Where .... Dare

4. The Wild ....

5. Black ....

6. To Kill a ....

7. The .... Brief

8. Black .... Down

9. The .... Runner

10. Red ....

General Knowledge
Culture, Legends and Folk Tales

1. What birds are known in fairy tales for delivering babies?

2. What species of bird is supposedly protecting the Crown and the Realm at the Tower of London?

3. What quality are owls reputed to have, which could be useful when seeking advice?

4. Which bird predicts changing fortunes according to how many you see – one for sorrow, two for joy, and so forth?

5. Which birds are supposed to predict bad weather by coming inland (although this is entirely false)?

6. According to the Bible, people are worth more than many of which bird? (Matthew 10: 31)

7. What birds are famous for their fidelity, and their sadness at losing a mate?

8. What birds are equated with thieves?

9. A swan is able to break your arm – true or false?

10. Where are all the baby pigeons?

Answers on page 247

PUZZLE 115

General Knowledge
Culture

1. Classic FM repeatedly polls its listeners, only to find that which Vaughan Williams piece is almost always its most popular tune?

2. Which bird, according to the Beatles' 1968 hit, was 'singing in the dead of night'?

3. Which birds are used as messengers and a postal service in the Harry Potter books by J K Rowling?

4. Which Hull-based indie rock band named after a bird had the hit single *Caravan of Love* in 1986?

5. Which famous comedian and entertainer was the original main presenter of the long-running wildlife series *Springwatch* on BBC?

6. To which bird did the romantic poet John Keats dedicate his famous 'ode' in around 1819?

7. According to the nursery rhyme, how many blackbirds were baked in a pie?

8. In the Black Forest, Germany, in the middle of the 18th century, they began mass-producing a special kind of clock, which eventually made its way over to Britain. What species of bird announced the hours?

9. Which famous British playwright wrote of 'the detested kite'?

10. Which famous British naturalist, in his *Natural History of Selborne*, published in 1789, is thought to have been the first to distinguish chiffchaff, willow warbler and wood warbler by song?

Answers on page 247

Mix and Match

Football Teams

Match the ornithological nickname with the British football team.
Some birds have more than one team.

Brighton and Hove Albion

Cheltenham Town

THE SEAGULLS

Cardiff City

THE EAGLES

Charlton Athletic

THE MAGPIES

Bristol City

THE ROBINS

Newcastle United

THE CANARIES

Norwich City

THE OWLS

Swansea City

THE BLUEBIRDS

Sheffield Wednesday

THE SWANS

Notts County

Swindon Town

Crystal Palace

Missing Words

Famous People

Can you fill in the birds, or words that sound like birds, to complete these names of famous people?

1. Graeme ....
Former English Test cricketer.

2. Alan ....
Fictional talk show host played by Steve Coogan.

3. ....-Z
American rapper.

4. Sheryl ....
American country singer.

5. John ....
English snooker player.

6. Ethan ....
American actor.

7. Taylor ....
American singer.

8. Chris ....
British singer.

9. Christopher ....
English architect, 17th–18th century.

10. Florence ....
English social reformer and nurse, 19th century.

General Knowledge
Christmas

1. In the Christmas song, the partridge is often referred to as sitting in a pear tree. Why is this unlikely?

2. Turkey is the traditional Christmas dinner in the UK, but where is the bird found in the wild?

3. *The Twelve Days of Christmas* song mentions 'seven swans a-swimming'. What species of swans occur in the UK at Christmas?

4. What does the 'colly' refer to in the 'four colly birds' in *The Twelve Days of Christmas*?

5. What highly significant event occurs in the week before Christmas, one that the birds themselves can detect?

6. Where does the nightingale find itself at Christmas?

7. What, according to most sources, is the connection between Christmas cards and robins?

8. Why would birds not want to experience a white Christmas?

9. Why might it now be difficult for 'my true love' to give to me 'two turtle doves'?

10. What wild bird song are you most likely to hear on Christmas Day?

Answers on page 248

CHAPTER EIGHT

A RARE SIGHT

Word Ladder

Complete each of these word ladders by writing a regular English word at each step. Each word must use the exact same letters in the same order as the word above, except with a single letter changed.

For example:

SHOW > SHOT > SOOT > SORT > SORE > MORE

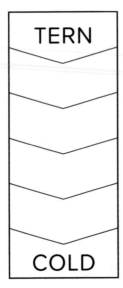

TERN

COLD

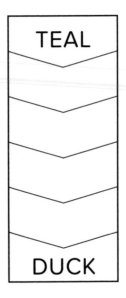

TEAL

DUCK

PUZZLE 120

What Bird Am I?

Can you figure out the species from the clues below?

I am rare in Britain but seen every year somewhere there, without fail.

I am a migrant to the southern half of Europe, wintering in Africa.

I breed in Africa, too, and east to the Himalayas.

I breed anywhere from lowlands to 4,000m (13,123ft), despite my name.

I eat flying insects, everything from ants to cicadas.

I have been recorded feeding at streetlights and in the dark, but I'm not nocturnal.

I collect feathers for my nest and bind them into a saucer shape with my saliva.

I sometimes mate in the air.

My colonies can persist for hundreds of years.

I can fly all day without stopping.

Did You Know?

The female red-legged partridge sometimes lays two clutches – she incubates one and the male incubates the other.

General Knowledge

These general knowledge questions are particularly tricky, so use the clues if you need some help!

1. What is the only officially extinct bird on the British List?

2. What is the only flightless bird on the British List?

3. Who was Vigo, who appeared in British skies in 2020?

4. Which species was not recorded in Britain until about 1953, but is now a common suburban bird?

5. What was particularly unusual about the appearance of the spotted sandpiper, an American bird, in 1975?

6. What rare seabird delighted watchers at Bempton Cliffs in Yorkshire, for much of 2021 and 2022?

7. The golden-winged warbler, a gorgeous American sprite, has only ever turned up in Britain on one occasion, in 1989. What was unusual about its location?

8. What links the following species: black woodpecker, Ural owl and hazel grouse?

9. What is the only bird officially listed as Critically Endangered that you have a reasonable chance of seeing in Britain in the late summer?

10. What links red-flanked bluetail, Pallas's warbler and Blyth's reed warbler, among others?

Clues:

1. It's a seabird
2. It's a seabird
3. It's a bird of prey
4. It's a garden bird
5. It's more than one bird
6. It's a seabird with a long wing-span
7. A supermarket
8. Lacking
9. It's a seabird from the Mediterranean
10. Regularity of appearance in the UK

PUZZLE 122

Codeword

Solve the following codeword and then rearrange the shaded squares to reveal a two-word term that the RSPB uses for UK birds in most urgent need of help. A codeword is a coded crossword in which every letter has been replaced by a number, indicated by the small digits in the top left corner of each crossword square.

As a further clue, the puzzle also contains two birds that fall under the heading of the term hidden in the shaded squares.

Mix and Match

Where Do They Come From?

As far as birds are concerned, the British Isles are situated almost in the centre of the world, and we receive birds from all points of the compass. Can you match the rare bird with its point of origin?

PALLAS'S SANDGROUSE

                            Caribbean

WHITE-CROWNED
BLACK WHEATEAR   Mountains of Europe

ALLEN'S GALLINULE   Central Asia

WALLCREEPER   Tropical Africa

PURPLE SWAMPHEN   Far Eastern Asia

AQUATIC WARBLER   Eastern Europe

MAGNIFICENT
FRIGATEBIRD   Southern Europe

                           North Africa

IVORY GULL

                           Arctic Ocean

NORTHERN
MOCKINGBIRD   USA

SIBERIAN BLUE ROBIN

PUZZLE 124

True or False?

	True	False
1. The lammergeier, recorded for the first time in Britain in 2019, is a vulture that specialises in feeding on bones.		
2. The spotted nutcracker, a bird found in the forests and mountains of Central and Northern Europe, inspired Tchaikovsky's ballet The Nutcracker, completed in 1892.		
3. The little bustard, an extreme rarity in Britain but found as close as France, makes a display sound resembling human flatulence.		
4. The Egyptian vulture, recorded twice in Britain in the 19th century, is famous for its revolting diet, which includes human faeces.		
5. The yellow-billed cuckoo, a great rarity from the US, builds its own nest and incubates its own eggs.		
6. The sooty tern is a tropical deep-ocean species that, unlike other terns, dives well underwater and chases fish while immersed.		
7. The hawk owl, a rare visitor from the north, is unusual for an owl in going to sleep at night.		
8. The Acadian flycatcher is so hard to identify that, when one turned up in Kent in 2015, it was only identified by DNA analysis of a feather.		
9. While the commonly occurring reed warbler is one of the main hosts of the common cuckoo in Britain, the great reed warbler is one of the main hosts of the great spotted cuckoo.		
10. One of the favourite foods of the snowy owl is lemmings.		

Answers on page 251

Wordsearch

Hard to See

Some birds are hard to spot. Find 18 words describing why this is, hidden in the letter grid. The words can read horizontally, vertically or diagonally, forwards or backwards.

```
D U U I T L U E H I D D E N V
S L A N O I T P E C X E I A S
U N C O M M O N O C I R N C N
D A C E V A S I V E C E F E N
C I N I E S R A P S A G R O D
H L M M D R L T D T M N E A E
E W A I I A E E A N O A Q P S
G L I N T N R T E N U D U C I
D D U T D E R O R I F N E I U
E E C S H E S E P E L E N I G
A D U V I D S A V S A R T N S
E M E R Y V R T N N G T T E I
S R C C H A E A I T E Y I S D
E O A V S R I A W N D N V N Q
Y I N R U N A E E N E U N T G
```

CAMOUFLAGED	EVASIVE	SHY
CLANDESTINE	EXCEPTIONAL	SPARSE
COY	HIDDEN	SPORADIC
DISGUISED	INFREQUENT	TIMID
ELUSIVE	RARE	UNCOMMON
ENDANGERED	RETREATING	WITHDRAWN

PUZZLE 126

General Knowledge

Stunners

The following questions are all about some of the most
beautiful of all the rare birds that turn up in the UK.

1. What is the favourite food of the waxwing?

2. What, according to birdwatchers, is often the best place to see a
   waxwing when it comes to the UK in the winter?

3. What does a bee-eater usually do before eating a bee or delivering
   food to its young?

4. What are the main two colours of the male golden oriole?

5. The roller, a relative of kingfishers and bee-eaters, is a rare but
   regular visitor to Britain. How does it get its name?

6. Several beautiful members of the shrike family are found in Europe.
   For what unusual feeding trait are they famous?

7. What gorgeous mountain-living sprite with bright red, white and
   black wings has a flight that is often compared to a butterfly's?

8. What does a hoopoe do when it is alarmed?

9. And why is the hoopoe so named?

10. What beautiful European bird, a delicacy in France, was reputedly
    the last meal of the late president of France, François Mitterrand?

Answers on page 251

PUZZLE 127

Odd One Out

From the following lists of birds, see if you can find the odd one out. There is a broad category for each to help you.

1. Habitat

a. *Alpine accentor*

b. *Citril finch*

c. *Bee-eater*

d. *Wallcreeper*

2. Origin

a. *Forster's tern*

b. *Blackburnian warbler*

c. *Summer tanager*

d. *Pallas's warbler*

3. Plumage

a. *Ivory gull*

b. *Snowy owl*

c. *Ross's gull*

d. *Ross's goose*

4. Affiliation

a. *Stilt sandpiper*

b. *Curlew sandpiper*

c. *Black-winged stilt*

d. *Black-winged curlew*

5. Lifestyle

a. *Sooty tern*

b. *Chimney swift*

c. *Alpine swift*

d. *Red-rumped swallow*

6. Feeding method

a. *Blue-winged teal*

b. *Harlequin duck*

c. *King eider*

d. *Surf scoter*

7. Feeding Method

a. *Rough-legged buzzard*

b. *Lesser kestrel*

c. *Belted kingfisher*

d. *Roller*

8. Physical Feature

a. *Red-billed tropicbird*

b. *Fan-tailed warbler (Zitting cisticola)*

c. *Long-tailed skua*

d. *Red-rumped swallow*

9. Habitat

a. *Pine grosbeak*

b. *Western olivaceous warbler*

c. *Two-barred crossbill*

d. *Nutcracker*

10. Diet

a. *Short-toed eagle*

b. *Red-footed falcon*

c. *Cliff swallow*

d. *Masked shrike*

PUZZLE 128

Mix and Match

Whose Bird?

A large number of birds on the British List are named after people.
Can you match the person with the bird?

GULL	Peter Gustaf Tengmalm
PETREL	Paolo Savi
WARBLER	James Clark Ross
SANDGROUSE	Thomas Bewick
BUNTING	Robert Swinhoe
OWL	Morten Thrane Brünnich
EIDER	Peter Simon Pallas
SANDPIPER	Philipp Jakob Cretzschmar
SWAN	Georg Wilhelm Steller
GUILLEMOT	Spencer Fullerton Baird

Crossword

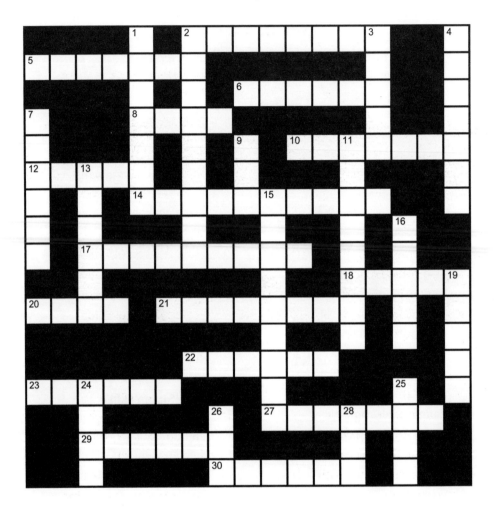

Across

2. Scottish archipelago where green-winged teals might be spotted (8)
5. A bird's feathers (7)
6. Perma-frozen ground, where American wigeons may breed (6)
8. Exceptional or infrequent (4)
10. Large area of Russia where long-tailed skuas nest (7)
12. Iberian country where penduline tits breed (5)
14. Having three sides, as the bill of a surf scoter (10)
17. Latest month of the year that black kites have been spotted in Britain (9)
18. North's opposite; the direction of many winter migrations from Britain (5)
20. Blue-green; type of freshwater duck (4)
21. Young; adolescent (8)
22. North American country where white-billed divers breed (6)
23. Season associated with warmth (6)
27. Scandinavian country where gull-billed terns breed (7)
29. An alpine swift's wing is shaped like this curved cropping tool (6)
30. Score; estimated number of ring-necked ducks that visit Britain each year (6)

Down

1. Any bird appearing outside its normal migratory range (7)
2. Enigmatic or reticent, as a ferruginous duck (9)
3. Male duck (5)
4. Condiment; shade of yellow, as a buff-breasted sandpiper's legs are (7)
7. Rural or bucolic; species of bunting (6)
9. Number of aquatic warblers seen in Britain each year, on average (3)
11. Inland body of water where rose-coloured starlings breed, bordering Russia (5, 3)
13. US State visited by migrating pectoral sandpipers (6)
15. Large North Atlantic island where Arctic redpolls may breed before migration (9)
16. Shed old feathers (5)
19. Stay in one place while flying, as a red-footed falcon does when hunting (5)
24. Face covering; bird feature that is black on a woodchat shrike (4)
25. Amphibian eaten by glossy ibises (4)
26. Glossy black colour, like the underwing of a Siberian stonechat (3)
28. Month when citrine wagtails might be spotted in Britain (3)

Answers on page 253

Anagrams

These are all birds on the British List. Can you work out any of these species from their anagrams?

1. Few tailspin

———— — ————

2. Brian's hurt, he is

———————— ——————

3. Bob boy worn

————— —————

4. No car, we imagine

———————— ——————

5. Our moving end

——————— ————

6. Dearest weather

————— ————————

7. Untitled pine

——————— ———

8. Lap nectar? O, nice!

————— —————————

9. No square choc

——————— —————

10. 'E's talking aloud

———— — ———————— ————

Missing Words

Place Names

Lots of Britain's birds are named after places – countries, states, regions and continents. Can you name the place and the rare bird named after it?

1. North African country on the Nile river.

_____ nightjar or vulture

2. State in the USA whose capital is famous for its country music.

_____ warbler

3. Eastern European historical region that also gives its name to spotty dogs.

_____ pelican

4. European country beloved of holidaymakers.

_____ sparrow

5. American city in Maryland with terrifying crime rate.

_____ oriole

6. Enormous lake in Russia, the world's deepest and oldest, containing nearly a quarter of the world's surface freshwater.

_____ teal

7. Large landlocked sea, bordered by Iran and Kazakhstan, among other countries.

_____ gull, plover or tern

8. Mountain range in Central Europe.

_____ swift or accentor

9. Name for the peninsula in Europe that incorporates Spain and Portugal.

_____ chiffchaff

10. Island in mid-Atlantic that is a British Overseas Territory.

_____ frigatebird

Answers on page 253

Fitword

Can you place all of these birds that the RSPB deems 'rarities' into the grid, crossword style? **Place only the words in bold**, and place each word individually even if both words in a name are highlighted in bold.

Alpine swift; American wigeon; aquatic **warbler; Arctic** redpoll; **Balearic** shearwater; **Caspian gull;** common **rosefinch; dusky** warbler; **glossy ibis; great** shearwater; **Kentish** plover; **lesser scaup; ortolan** bunting; **Siberian stonechat; surf scoter;** woodchat **shrike.**

What Bird Am I?

The following are brief descriptions of birds rare in Britain. Can you match the bird with its description?

___. Ivory gull   ___. Black-winged stilt

___. Red-backed shrike   ___. Eleonora's falcon

___. Rose-coloured starling   ___. Spoonbill

___. Short-toed treecreeper   ___. Pallas's sandgrouse

1. I am shaped like a bird very common in your garden, but I should be viewed through rose-tinted spectacles. I am an eastern invader, usually turning up in midsummer.

2. I come from Central Asia, where I have a nomadic existence in arid areas. I am unusual for my habit of visiting water holes and wetting my breast plumage to bring water to my chicks.

3. I come from the High Arctic, where life is hard. I am one of the very few birds with completely white plumage (when adult). I am often seen eating the carcases and faeces of whales and seals.

4. I am famous – and named – for my very long, shocking pink legs, which enable me to wade in saline water. I am very noisy, even more so than my relative the avocet.

5. I am an extraordinary colonial bird of prey of the Mediterranean and Atlantic. I breed on cliffs and islands and start breeding very late, to feed my young on migratory birds moving south.

6. I was once a relatively common and familiar bird over England and Wales, but I suffered a decline for 100 years and 1989 was the first year for millennia that I didn't breed in Britain. I regularly impale prey for storage on thorns and other sharp points.

7. I am famous for my spatula-shaped bill, which I use to help me to catch fish in shallow water, using touch to detect them. After many years of absence, I am now breeding in Britain again.

8. I am very similar to a common British bird, but I replace it in lowland wooded areas of Europe. I am noisier than my counterpart, but almost impossible to distinguish from it.

Answers on page 254

Multiple Choice

Seabirds

1. Which rare seabird has relatively the lightest bones of any species in the world, contributing only five per cent of its body weight?

   a. *Tropicbird*   **b.** *Frigatebird*

   c. *Pelican*   **d.** *Albatross*

2. Which rare seabird is known to follow scent trails by flying in a zigzagging path across the ocean?

   a. *Sooty tern*   **b.** *Red-billed tropicbird*

   c. *Wilson's petrel*   **d.** *Tufted puffin*

3. Which rare seabird specialises in preying on flying fish, which it catches as they flee predators below?

   a. *Sooty tern*   **b.** *Great shearwater*

   c. *Wilson's petrel*   **d.** *Black-browed albatross*

4. What is the only member of the cormorant family, apart from our two breeding species (great cormorant and shag) to have been recorded in Britain?

   a. *Pelagic cormorant*   **b.** *Pygmy cormorant*

   c. *Socotra cormorant*   **d.** *Double-crested cormorant*

5. What is unusual about the only record of Atlantic yellow-nosed albatross in Britain?

   a. *It was seen from a boat in the North Atlantic, just inside Britain's territorial waters*

   b. *It was seen on a boating lake far inland*

   c. *It died a few minutes after being found on a beach*

   d. *It was seen just a day before the new millennium, in 1899*

6. What happened to the red-footed booby, found on the beach at St Leonards-on-Sea in September 2016, the first record for Britain?

   a. *It was taken back to the Caribbean but died before release*

   b. *It flew off and was seen again in the same place the following year*

   c. *It was kept in care and released and was last seen consorting with a gannet in Scotland*

   d. *It was taken back to the Caribbean and is part of a breeding colony in Puerto Rico*

7. What was unusual about the record of Ascension Frigatebird, which was found moribund on a loch in the Inner Hebrides in 1953?

   a. *The body was given to the Queen to celebrate the Coronation*

   b. *The body was burnt in a fire in Edinburgh Museum a year later*

   c. *It remains the oldest accepted record of a bird in Britain just from a photograph*

   d. *It was misidentified as another species of frigatebird for 50 years*

8. Which rare seabird was first claimed for Britain in 1698, but it wasn't until 2001, more than 300 years later, that there was a definite sighting near the Isles of Scilly?

   a. *Brown booby*   **b.** *Red-billed tropicbird*

   c. *Bermuda petrel*   **d.** *White-vented storm petrel*

9. Which seabird is only seen occasionally in Britain itself, but the majority of the world population breeds in British Overseas Territories?

   a. *South polar skua*   **b.** *Black-browed albatross*

   c. *Sooty tern*   **d.** *Wilson's petrel*

10. What is unusual about the record of Britain's first giant petrel seen twice, in Durham and Northumberland, in 2019?

   a. *The observers were drunk when it was initially seen*

   b. *It was seen on the same day as a black-browed albatross*

   c. *It couldn't be assigned a species, so isn't officially on the British List*

   d. *It was seen both from land and at sea on the same day*

Word Circle

Rearrange the letters in the circle below to reveal a two-word bird of prey which has a well-known, rufous cousin. You might also find a small, dabbling duck. Then, how many words can you find that use the centre letter plus two or more of the other letters? No letter may be used more times than it appears within the circle.

PUZZLE 136

General Knowledge

Across the Pond

How well do you know your American birds? These questions are all about species that have been recorded here but are really denizens of the New World.

1. Which species is notorious for being a brood parasite of many North American birds, even threatening the populations of some of them?

2. Which wader (shorebird in the US) shares a name with a popular British high society magazine?

3. Which Northern American bird is famous for its habit of imitating a wide variety of other birds in its song?

4. Which wildfowl breeds in the High Arctic of North America, but is most famous for its winter gatherings of vast numbers, leading to its common name?

5. Which much-beloved American bird has a red breast, leading to it being named after a familiar British species?

6. Which songbird, named after a colour of the rainbow, was the subject of remarkable studies in which young birds were proved to navigate by the stars having been raised in a planetarium?

7. Which popular aerial songbird has spawned a whole industry for householders putting up elaborate boxes?

8. The only woodpecker to have crossed the Atlantic, which species is named after its habit of drinking from holes made in the bark of trees and is considered a pest in some places?

9. Which thrush, roughly equivalent to our song thrush, has one of the most glorious songs of any American bird?

10. Which American wader or shorebird, recorded at least five times in Britain up to 1887, is now almost certainly extinct?

Answers on page 255

Half Anagrams

A large number of rarities in Britain seem either to be warblers (of various kinds), gulls or sandpipers. Can you unscramble the half-names?

Gulls

1. Strap a bone

_ _ _ _ _ _ _ _ _ , _ _

2. S.E. Basin

_ _ _ _ _ _ , _ _

3. By a salt deck

_ _ _ _ _ _ - _ _ _ _ _ _ _

Sandpipers

4. Stale

_ _ _ _ _

5. Meat pies m'lad

_ _ _ _ _ _ _ _ _ _ _ _ _

6. Late crop

_ _ _ _ _ _ _ _

Warblers

7. Reincite

_ _ _ _ _ _ _ _

8. Call one date

_ _ _ _ _ _ _ _ _ _ _

9. I am along

_ _ _ _ _ _ _ _

10. Pay came

_ _ _ _ _ _ _

PUZZLE 138

Pathfinder

Can you find nine birds, all rarely spotted but with colours in their names, hidden in the grid below? All of the birds have two-word names, and sometimes one of those two words is hyphenated too.

The start of the path is marked, at the top left, ending at the shaded square. Find a path that visits every grid square exactly once each, spelling them out as it goes. The path can only travel horizontally or vertically between squares. Avoid the two squares with binoculars, just as the birds themselves might!

G	R	E	N	G	R	E	I	S	H	W	A
W	N	E	O	C	L	E	N	C	R	E	R
I	A	L	L	E	A	F	T	I	●●	L	B
N	E	T	S	S	E	D	R	N	G	T	A
G	E	D	E	O	T	●●	I	I	Y	N	W
L	E	Y	R	O	F	E	N	L	P	I	T
L	G	S	W	E	D	W	A	R	I	P	
O	E	I	H	R	R	A	T	E	R	U	O
W	L	T	I	P	E	G	S	D	C	O	L
U	R	E	P	I	A	T	O	S	E	I	P
M	D	S	D	L	I	V	R	T	I	P	D
P	E	A	N	O	L	E	B	A	C	K	E

What Bird Am I?

So Near. . .

The following species occur near the UK but have never been seen here, despite their proximity. Can you identify the bird from the description?

1. I breed in large colonies in the Camargue and other parts of Europe. I usually feed upside down and I feed my young on a kind of milk.

2. I probably breed closer to the UK than any other unrecorded bird – in the Netherlands, Belgium and France. I am named after my (lack of) colour and I feed mainly on ants.

3. I live in high mountains – in fact, I have been found in the Himalayas perched at a greater altitude than any other bird. I often live in noisy flocks.

4. I am a relative midget in my family, and I breed in Eastern Europe on freshwater lakes. In common with others, I hold my wings out to dry after feeding.

5. I am another high-mountain species that skiers might see in winter, often feeding on scraps at resorts above 2,000m (6,562ft). I have the right plumage colour for the altitude. Amazingly, I've been found in the lowlands of Sweden and even the Canary Islands, but not in Britain.

6. I breed in Spain and Central Asia, on saline lakes. I am so rare that a North American import was eradicated from Britain in order to protect me.

7. I might be a dream for birdwatchers, but I breed as far north as central France and am expanding, having been no closer than North Africa in the 1970s. I am a small raptor that feeds on rodents while hovering, often at dusk.

8. I am a raptor from Eastern Europe, the smaller of two closely related species. I am migratory, wintering in Africa. I eat mainly small mammals.

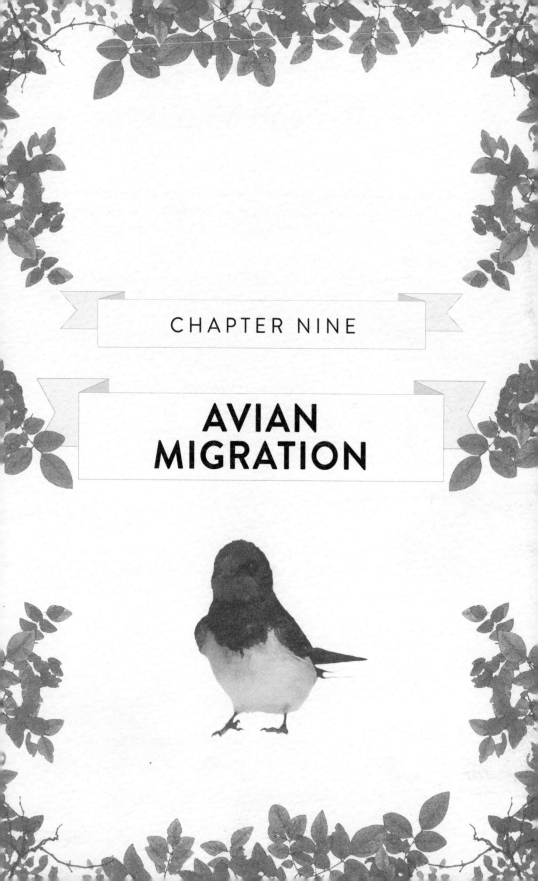

CHAPTER NINE

AVIAN MIGRATION

Mix and Match

Month by Month

We are all familiar with the comings and goings of birds during the year. But can you match the annual ornithological event with the month in which it usually happens?

JANUARY	The first redwings, fieldfares and wild geese begin to arrive in force to spend the winter in the UK.
FEBRUARY	This is probably the main month of moulting for most of the birds of Britain.
MARCH	International Dawn Chorus Day is celebrated.
APRIL	The RSPB's Big Garden Birdwatch is held.
MAY	Broods of tits are disgorged in vast quantities from the production lines that are their nests.
JUNE	Robins start singing again after their summer break.
JULY	Masses of starlings are gathering in their communal roosts at the end of the year's shortest days.
AUGUST	
SEPTEMBER	Song thrushes usually begin to sing their territorial songs.
OCTOBER	Traditionally, this is the month when the highest numbers of wild ducks are counted in Britain.
NOVEMBER	The first sand martins arrive in Britain.
DECEMBER	The first cuckoo is heard calling in Britain.
	The last swifts normally depart from Britain.

Answers on page 257

Fitword

Can you place all of these resident, non-migratory birds into the grid, crossword style? Ignore any spaces.

Five-letter word
Crane

Seven-letter words
Coal tit
Dunnock
Kestrel
Mallard
Red kite
Skylark

Eight-letter words
Great tit
Nuthatch
Pheasant
Woodcock

Nine-letter words
Cormorant
Red grouse
Rock pipit
Stock dove

Ten-letter words
Crested tit
Tufted duck

Eleven-letter words
Little grebe
Meadow pipit

General Knowledge

1. What birds have the longest migration from the UK?

2. What other unusual distinction does this bird have as a result of its movements?

3. What wader species undertakes the longest non-stop migration in the world?

4. What is the official name given to the stopover sites used by birds to take a long rest during migration?

5. What is the main source of energy for migratory birds?

6. On which journey do birds travel faster – outward journeys (when birds in the UK migrate to their wintering areas) or return journeys?

7. Name two reasons why birds might migrate at night.

8. What is unusual about the migration of the swift?

9. What term is used by excited birdwatchers to describe an event when many birds touch down at a certain location, usually owing to adverse weather conditions?

10. When migrating, what do birds of prey avoid as much as possible?

Wordsearch

Can you find the following birds, all of which have locations or nationalities in their names, in the wordsearch grid? Only the CAPITALISED words are to be found – ignore the words in lower-case letters. Words can read horizontally, vertically or diagonally, forwards or backwards.

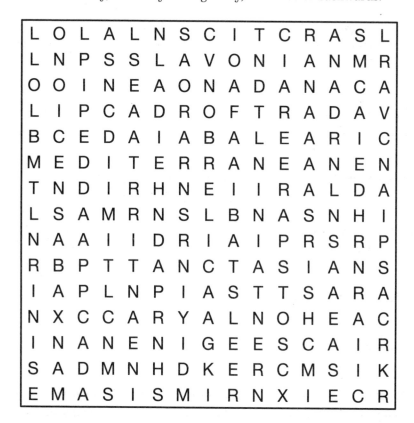

```
L O L A L N S C I T C R A S L
L N P S S L A V O N I A N M R
O O I N E A O N A D A N A C A
L I P C A D R O F T R A D A V
B C E D A I A B A L E A R I C
M E D I T E R R A N E A N E N
T N D I R H N E I I R A L D A
L S A M R N S L B N A S N H I
N A A I I D R I A I P R S R P
R B P T T A N C T A S I A N S
I A P L N P I A S T T S A R A
N X C C A R Y A L N O H E A C
I N A N E N I G E E S C A I R
S A D M N H D K E R C M S I K
E M A S I S M I R N X I E C R
```

AMERICAN wigeon	DARTFORD warbler	MANX shearwater
ARCTIC skua	EGYPTIAN goose	MEDITERRANEAN gull
BALEARIC shearwater	ICELAND gull	SCOTTISH crossbill
CANADA goose	KENTISH plover	SIBERIAN stonechat
CASPIAN gull	LAPLAND bunting	SLAVONIAN grebe

Mix and Match

Do you know where our birds go in winter? There are ten locations
for British breeding birds marked on this map – can you match
the species to its wintering area?

—. BLACKCAP

—. WILLOW WARBLER

—. RING OUZEL

—. MANX SHEARWATER

—. SWALLOW

—. KITTIWAKE

—. ARCTIC TERN

—. LESSER WHITETHROAT

—. COMMON TERN

—. GOLDFINCH

Multiple Choice

Migration

1. In many cases, birds from northern regions migrate further south than birds setting off from more temperate regions. What is the term for this?

   a. *Lopsided migration* **b.** *Differential migration*

   c. *Leapfrog migration* **d.** *Enhanced migration*

2. In many species, males and females, or adults and young, make differing journeys, with different destinations. What is the term for this?

   a. *Sexist migration* **b.** *Differential migration*

   c. *Stage migration* **d.** *Familial migration*

3. Which of these species learns its migration from its parents?

   a. *Crane* **b.** *Mallard*

   c. *Cuckoo* **d.** *Redstart*

4. Which species of pipit breeds in the mountains of Europe and then, peculiarly, migrates NORTH to Britain in the AUTUMN?

   a. *Meadow pipit* **b.** *Tree pipit*

   c. *Rock pipit* **d.** *Water pipit*

5. PARTIAL MIGRATION is a very confusing phenomenon among many bird species – but what is it?

   a. *It is when different individuals from the same regional population either migrate or stay put.*

   b. *It is when a bird on migration decides not to continue all the way to its original destination.*

   c. *It is when a species exhibits both populations that are wholly resident and those that are wholly migratory.*

   d. *It is when a bird migrates in one direction, pauses and then goes off in a different direction.*

6. Sometimes a bird follows quite a different route on its outbound migration (from breeding to wintering areas) compared to its return migration. What is the term for this?

a. *Differential migration* **b.** *Sling migration*

c. *Loop migration* **d.** *Drift migration*

7. Many species of ducks, geese and swans come to Britain to spend the winter but which one spends the summer here and then migrates south to winter in Africa?

a. *Gadwall* **b.** *Garganey*

c. *Egyptian goose* **d.** *Shoveler*

8. The warblers are a famously migratory group, but which of these species doesn't normally migrate to Africa?

a. *Dartford warbler* **b.** *Sedge warbler*

c. *Wood warbler* **d.** *Garden warbler*

9. Which of these birds typically migrates by day, as opposed to night?

a. *Spotted flycatcher* **b.** *Redstart*

c. *Redwing* **d.** *Swallow*

10. Under normal conditions, which is the latest of these summer migrants to arrive?

a. *Sand martin* **b.** *Reed warbler*

c. *Cuckoo* **d.** *Spotted flycatcher*

Did You Know?

The house martin goes south in autumn to winter in Africa but, amazingly, nobody knows exactly where it goes. Millions of house martins simply disappear.

PUZZLE 146

Codeword

Solve the following codeword and then rearrange the shaded squares to reveal a resident bird that, as far as its British and Irish populations are concerned, does not migrate. A codeword is a coded crossword in which every letter has been replaced by a number, indicated by the small digits in the top left corner of each crossword square.

As a further clue, the puzzle also contains two additional resident birds.

Mix and Match

Tracked Migration Routes

In recent years, scientists have tracked the routes of a number of British birds to reveal exactly where they go in the winter. Can you match the species with the tracked route?

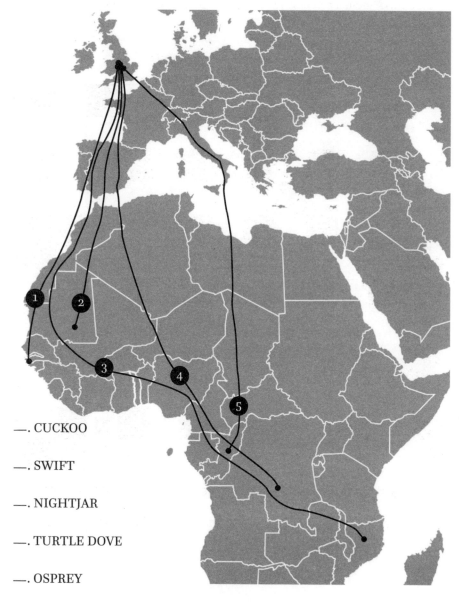

—. CUCKOO

—. SWIFT

—. NIGHTJAR

—. TURTLE DOVE

—. OSPREY

True or False?

Finding the Way

One of the great wonders of science, let alone bird biology, is how birds manage to navigate their way around the world. Here are a few statements about it – spot the true from the false.

	True	False
1. Birds know what time of year it is by an internal clock controlled by the length of the day.		
2. All birds seek out older individuals and members of the same species to help them to take the right route in migration.		
3. Birds using the sun can only migrate in the morning, because otherwise they get lost when it moves across the sky.		
4. Birds migrating at night usually set off at sunset so that they know which direction is west.		
5. In an unusual experiment, it was found that pigeons can find their way around by following smells.		
6. When migrating at night, it has been shown that birds can remember every single star in the sky.		
7. Birds can tell how far north or south they are by magnetic fields.		
8. Birds can probably predict storms because they are sensitive to atmospheric pressure.		
9. Mobile phone masts are a problem for birds migrating because they give off unexpected magnetic signals.		
10. Birds use landmarks and can recognise features such as roundabouts, car parks and pubs.		

Mix and Match

Song Calendar

Match the species to a month in which it can be heard regularly singing. You can only use each species once, and there's no robin to help you! And yes, everything sings in April and May.

JANUARY	Great tit
FEBRUARY	Chiffchaff
MARCH	Mistle thrush
JUNE	Yellowhammer
JULY	Blackbird
AUGUST	Tawny owl
SEPTEMBER	Wren
OCTOBER	Woodpigeon
NOVEMBER	Dipper
DECEMBER	Reed warbler

Word Ladder

Complete each of these word ladders by writing a regular English word at each step. Each word must use the exact same letters in the same order as the word above, except with a single letter changed.

For example:

SHOW > SHOT > SOOT > SORT > SORE > MORE

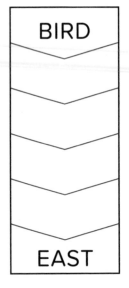

BIRD

EAST

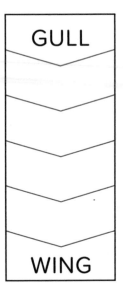

GULL

WING

What Bird Am I?

Personal Timekeeping

Can you match the bird in the list below to its journey, average UK arrival and departure times, plus the odd clue?

___. Sand martin   ___. Redwing/fieldfare

___. Swift   ___. Pink-footed goose

___. Cuckoo

1. Arrives in the UK in early May and stays only until August, leaving for West Africa and then Central Africa.

2. Arrives in the UK in March, usually the second week, leaving early, often by the end of August, and travelling to West Africa, south of the Sahara for the winter.

3. Arrives in noisy flocks in the UK in October from Greenland and Iceland, often in a single stretch from the latter, then departs north by April.

4. Arrives from Northern Europe in October in flocks, usually at night, appearing in large numbers and then spreading out all over the countryside to look for berries. Often strays into gardens before leaving quietly in March and April.

5. Arrives with a song in April, the first ones celebrated in *The Times* newspaper. After being noisy, all but disappears from the consciousness, the adults leaving the country in July and the young in August, their destination tropical Central Africa.

Answers on page 262

General Knowledge

Berried Treasure

If you're a bird, one of the things you will quickly become aware of is that certain foods are only available at certain times of year. Here are some questions to test your general knowledge!

1. What is the name given to the crop of beech and other trees that begins to ripen in October and November?

2. Name a month when ivy produces its berries – a time when most other berries are used up.

3. What is the worst time for most birds to find food in the wild, the so-called 'hungry gap'?

4. What's unusual about the colour of mistletoe berries, which are available between October and April?

5. There can be 10,000 of these on a single large oak tree, which is easily enough to feed many families of tits in early summer. What are they?

6. Which bird often continues breeding late into the summer, often to August, because of the abundance of thistle seeds?

7. On hot summer days, often after a period of rain, several sorts of birds, including gulls, starlings, sparrows and swallows, often swoop around excitedly just above rooftop height. What are they eating?

8. Rooks often nest very early in the year. It is thought that this is because it is easier for the parents to find a type of food that is in the soil. What food?

9. Many birds change their diets from one season to another. This is particularly stark in the case of tits. What is their main food in summer, then in winter?

10. Sparrowhawks tend to nest fairly late in the year – why is this?

Answers on page 262

Word Circle

Rearrange the letters in the circle below to reveal a bird that is
described as 'highly sedentary', although it will move to new
locations in poor weather. Then, how many other words can you
find that use the centre letter plus two or more of the other letters?
No letter may be used more times than it appears within the circle.

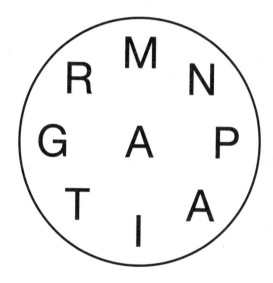

PUZZLE 154

Multiple Choice

Weather

It is easy to forget that birds live outside and are exposed to all weathers, without recourse to overcoats and umbrellas. Here are some questions about birds and weather.

1. Other than lightning, what natural meteorological event can actually kill birds directly?

    a. *Thunder*   **b.** *Rain*

    c. *Snow*   **d.** *Hail*

2. What species of bird is thought to be able to detect a weather front from hundreds of miles away, probably by the drop in flying insect numbers?

    a. *Lesser black-backed gull*   **b.** *Swift*

    c. *Willow warbler*   **d.** *Chaffinch*

3. Why is it thought to be better to align the entrance of a nest box away from south?

    a. *The sun could overheat eggs or chicks*

    b. *The sun may damage nestlings' eyes*

    c. *It affects the young birds' ability to orientate*

    d. *The sun damages the nestlings' feathers*

4. If you are a lapwing, which of these winter meteorological conditions is especially bad news?

    a. *Wind*   **b.** *Rain*

    c. *Sleet*   **d.** *Frost*

5. In winter, what's the biggest problem facing kingfishers?

    a. *Fast-flowing water*   **b.** *Wind*

    c. *Ice*   **d.** *Autumn leaves*

6. Kestrels have trouble hovering and hunting successfully at certain wind speeds. At what minimum speed, in metres per second, does the wind begin to cause this disruption?

a. *1m/s*   **b.** *10m/s*

c. *15m/s*   **d.** *20m/s*

7. Swifts, swallows and martins often fly lower down, close to the ground when it is raining or cloudy. Why is this?

a. *The air is denser low down and it's easier to fly*

b. *They are able to see better*

c. *The only insects available are close to the ground*

d. *They are avoiding dangerous turbulence*

8. Why is a spring or summer drought a particular problem for blackbirds and song thrushes?

a. *They overheat very easily*

b. *It's too bright for birds that usually forage in the shade*

c. *It makes them ill*

d. *Worms are harder to reach in the baked ground surface*

9. What conditions have been found to reduce the calling of tawny owls at night?

a. *Too warm*   **b.** *Too cold*

c. *Too wet*   **d.** *Too dry*

10. What is generally the best weather for migrating?

a. *Anticyclone*   **b.** *Cold front*

c. *Storm*   **d.** *Snow*

Answers on page 263

PUZZLE 155

Crossword

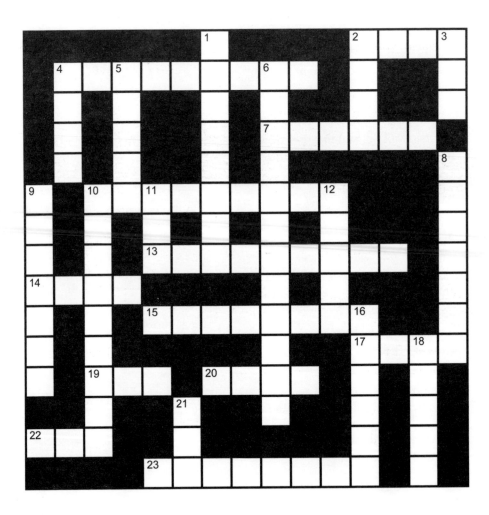

Across

2. At a fairly high temperature (4)

4. Vast expanse of land, such as Europe or Africa (9)

7. Typically cold season from which birds might migrate away (6)

10. Group of North Atlantic islands close to Iceland, where gannets may breed (3, 6)

13. Large North Atlantic island, where little auks may breed (9)

14. Unusual or infrequently spotted (4)

15. UK country where most British whimbrels breed (8)

17. Compass point associated with the rising sun (4)

19. The short-eared species of this nocturnal bird migrates as far south as the Mediterranean basin and even North Africa (3)

20. A bird's feathered forelimb; swifts sleep 'on' this (4)

22. Travel through the air, as a bird (3)

23. Permanent inhabitant; any non-migratory bird (8)

Down

1. Keep an 11 down warm before hatching (8)

2. Compass point opposite 17 across (4)

3. Chart or plan, used to show migratory routes (3)

4. Chilly; arctic (4)

5. Compass point; direction in which whitethroats migrate in April (5)

6. Large Canadian island where sooty shearwaters gather (12)

8. Any bird which travels from one place to another (7)

9. Any bird which has strayed outside its typical distribution (7)

10. Area which a bird might live in or defend (9)

11. Ovoid object laid by female birds (3)

12. European country where dotterels may travel during 7 across (5)

16. Abandon, as male gadwalls do to their nesting mates (6)

18. Compass point; direction in which nightjars fly in August and September (5)

21. Frozen water, sometimes perched on by Arctic terns (3)

Answers on page 263

True or False?

Migration is full of facts, figures and surprises. Can you tell which of the following statements is true or false?

	True	False
1. An albatross can fly further in a day than many birds do in a lifetime.		
2. Small, migrating birds such as warblers usually fly incredibly high when migrating, well above 5,000 m (16,400ft).		
3. In autumn, Britain almost empties of birds when all our migrants travel away.		
4. Some birds migrate by swimming, or even walking.		
5. Once they have started their migration, birds must avoid any mistakes. They cannot turn back or re-set.		
6. Once they've taken off, birds always fly for many hours on migration.		
7. Once it has achieved a migratory journey, a bird will always take the same route again.		
8. Once a bird has arrived in its winter quarters, it remains there the whole time.		
9. It is a great advantage for a small bird to fly at night, because the air is cooler and less dense, and there is less wind and turbulence.		
10. Birds that fly at night have special adaptations for night vision.		

Answers on page 264

Missing Words

Dangers

To migrate successfully is to overcome a series of potential dangers. Can you work out the hazard from the description and safely arrive at your destination?

Each successful answer moves you on one step towards home. A wrong answer and you're done for!

I am a migrant bird, about to fly.

1. First, I must make sure I have taken in enough _ _ _ to feed my journey. Otherwise, I will be in trouble.

2. It is the evening and I'm ready. I will check the sunset. I don't want to fly off in the _ _ _ _ _/_ _ _ _ _ _ _ _ _

3. I check the weather. I won't set off in the _ _ _ _

4. It seems to be clear, and I hope it will stay that way. I have a long _ _ _ crossing to make, and if the weather changes midway I could be in trouble.

5. I made it okay. The only hazard was on the far coast, where the _ _ _ _ _ from a building confused me.

6. I have fed well today, but I won't be going anywhere tonight. The _ _ _ _ has got up.

7. I tried to set off the night after, but I soon stopped. I couldn't see a thing because of the _ _ _

8. I was just landing after a good night's migrating, when we were all attacked by a _ _ _ _/ _ _ / _ _ _ _. I got away, but not everybody did.

9. Down in the Mediterranean today. I heard some bangs and several of my colleagues just blew up in a ball of feathers. They had been _ _ _ _

10. Bit grim now. All there is for miles around is sand, and no water. I hate these _ _ _ _ _ _ crossings.

11. Thank goodness, I've arrived. Instinct tells me that it's now time to _ _ _ _. If I go further, I might perish in the sea.

Multiple Choice

Warblers

Few bird families are so evocative of summer than warblers.
Almost all long-distance migrants, their noisy songs dominate
the breeding season. See if you can answer these multiple-choice
questions about our feathered friends.

1. Which warbler that breeds on heathlands is famous not for migrating, but for staying put?

   a. *Grasshopper warbler*   **b.** *Dartford warbler*

   c. *Garden warbler*   **d.** *Willow warbler*

2. Which common British species is famous for its East Siberian cousins flying 15,000 km (9,320 miles) from Siberia to East Africa to winter?

   a. *Willow warbler*   **b.** *Reed warbler*

   c. *Cetti's warbler*   **d.** *Garden warbler*

3. Which silvery-voiced warbler of northern and western oak woods disappears very soon after breeding and is rarely seen beyond August?

   a. *Chiffchaff*   **b.** *Wood warbler*

   c. *Blackcap*   **d.** *Sedge warbler*

4. Which metronomic-singing warbler is the first to arrive in Britain in the spring, and usually the last to leave?

   a. *Lesser whitethroat*   **b.** *Garden warbler*

   c. *Chiffchaff*   **d.** *Reed warbler*

5. Which marshland-edge warbler is very unusual for adopting a special diet in the autumn, bingeing on plum-reed aphids, which seem to propel it to West Africa in one go?

   a. *Sedge warbler*   **b.** *Chiffchaff*

   c. *Willow warbler*   **d.** *Marsh warbler*

6. Which now very rare warbler used to be the very last migrant bird to arrive in the summer, sometimes not appearing until June?

a. *Garden warbler* **b.** *Willow warbler*

c. *Lesser whitethroat* **d.** *Marsh warbler*

7. Which warbler has become famous for changing its migration? Individuals breeding in Central Europe always used to go to Spain and Portugal, but now often turn up in British gardens.

a. *Willow warbler* **b.** *Lesser whitethroat*

c. *Blackcap* **d.** *Wood warbler*

8. Which scratchy-voiced warbler suffered a huge crash in population in 1968, when 90 per cent of the population didn't return after being killed by a drought in sub-Saharan Africa? The recovery is still not complete today.

a. *Reed warbler* **b.** *Blackcap*

c. *Common whitethroat* **d.** *Garden warbler*

9. This warbler was once a very rare autumn visitor, but nowadays this breeding bird of Siberia is seen in significant numbers every year. What is it?

a. *Yellow-browed warbler* **b.** *Lesser whitethroat*

c. *Dartford warbler* **d.** *Marsh warbler*

10. In a famous experiment, individuals of this species kept in Europe in cages would flutter south-west in September, but this changed to south-east in October, mirroring their true journey in the wild and proving that migratory direction is built-in. Which species?

a. *Lesser whitethroat* **b.** *Reed warbler*

c. *Common whitethroat* **d.** *Garden warbler*

Answers on page 264

Pathfinder

Can you find eight birds, all of which might cross the Sahara Desert during migration, in the grid below? Starting at the shaded square, find a path that visits every grid square exactly once each, spelling them out as it goes. The path can only travel horizontally or vertically between squares, and should end at the star.

Note that one of the birds has two words, and one is hyphenated.

Q	U	A	I	N	C	H	A
A	E	I	H	T	H	G	T
T	E	L	W	I	N	I	N
E	E	B	W	O	G	A	L
R	C	O	R	L	L	A	E
A	R	C	N	R	E	W	S
K	S	P	Y	T	E	P	I
E	O	R	E	☆	T	I	P

PUZZLE 160

What Bird Am I?

Migrant

Can you identify the species from these statements
about its migration?

I usually migrate by day.

I tend to fly between 27 and 35 km/h (17–22 mph), with a maximum
speed of 56 km/h (35 mph).

I can fly 322 km (200 miles) a day.

I fly in groups or flocks.

I usually leave Britain in September.

I migrate down the French coast and turn left (east) at the Pyrenees,
following their northern slopes to the Mediterranean.

I cross the middle of the Sahara Desert.

My journey ends in South Africa.

My journey north can take as little as five weeks.

While migrating, I eat on the way, like a marathon runner!

Did You Know?

After breeding, British male goosanders go on a jolly.
They all pack off to Arctic Norway, leaving the
females and young behind!

What Bird Am I?

Personal Timekeeping

Can you match the bird in the list below to its journey, average arrival and departure times in the UK, plus the odd clue?

___. Shelduck

___. Manx shearwater

___. Puffin

___. Chiffchaff

___. Blackcap

1. Cheerful harbinger of spring, often arriving in woodlands in mid-March, then singing incessantly all summer long. Departs in late September and October for West Africa, but some stay or arrive to spend the winter in the south of the UK.

2. A chatty spring migrant, arriving on our shores in the first week of April and leaving in September and October for a modest movement to Spain and Portugal. In autumn, some arrive from Central Europe to bully other birds at feeding stations.

3. After a winter at sea, it returns to its breeding colonies on islands and headlands in March, remaining until late summer, when it often abruptly departs back to the sea, shedding the outer plates of its colourful bill.

4. A very unusual migrant. It would be resident in Britain, except that every summer, in July, adults travel overnight to the coast of Germany (Heligoland Bight) and spend a couple of months moulting, eventually returning by October.

5. Arrives in the UK in March, then in August it begins an incredible sweep of the oceans, wintering off South America.

ANSWERS

CHAPTER ONE

Great Garden Birds

PUZZLE 1 – Hidden Names

1. The siblings used to SPAR, ROW and argue all the time.
2. The sergeant said that his platoon had a pretty meaGRE ATTITude to hard work.
2. The homemade breW RENdered them virtually incapacitated!
4. I am still sMARTINg from the comments you made!
5. I didn't expect to see all those hippoS WALLOWing in the mud.
6. I personally found the movie Men in BLACK CAPtivating.
7. There is no doubt that members of the cluB LACK BIRDing experience.
8. It's nice to see the pole STAR LINGering in the sky.
9. She is a good organiser, and that's HER ONe good point, I think.
10. I'm not a great fan of your cROOKed nose, to be honest.

PUZZLE 2 – Pathfinder

	B	L	O	W	D	M
U	L	L	O	C	E	A
E	W	I	A	I	L	R
L	O	G	L	A	H	S
D	O	N	G	T	C	R
C	L	T	E	T	S	E
R	E	S	D	T	I	T

1. BLUE (tit)
2. WILLOW (tit)
3. COAL (tit)
4. GOLDCREST
5. LONG-TAILED (tit)
6. MARSH (tit)
7. CRESTED (tit)

Puzzle 3 – What Bird Am I? *Where and How Do I Feed in the Garden?*

1. Starling
2. Robin
3. Blackbird
4. Greenfinch
5. Magpie
6. Coal tit
7. Chaffinch
8. Tawny owl
9. Dunnock
10. Goldfinch

PUZZLE 4 – General Knowledge *Colours*

1. Pink-brown
2. Orange (red)
3. Chocolate-brown
   (with white eye-ring)
4. Orange (yellow)
5. Blue

6. Pale pink
7. Blue
8. Pink
9. Black
10. Grey-green

PUZZLE 5 – Wordsearch *Garden Birds*

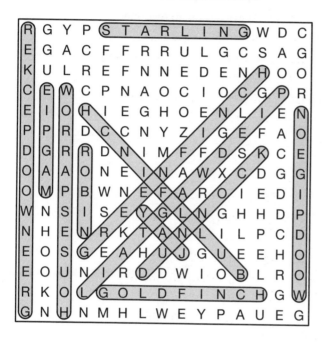

PUZZLE 6 – True or False?

1. TRUE
2. TRUE
3. TRUE
4. FALSE – it's a quarter of a second!
5. TRUE
6. FALSE – it spots insects by eye and opens its mouth to snap them up.
7. TRUE

8. FALSE – not true at all. It's a complete fabrication.
9. FALSE – no, the bird beats its bill against bark only to make the noise, not a hole. When excavating, the sound is quite different, not as fast or sonorous.
10. TRUE

PUZZLE 7 – General Knowledge

1. It can bash snails against a hard surface to break their shells.
2. The black stripe down the yellow breast is broader and goes down further.
3. Thistle seeds.
4. Starling.
5. The main difference is that it isn't in a cavity. It is also domed and put together with cobwebs.
6. A flimsy nest made up of sticks, usually in a bush or tree.
7. Its colouring – pie usually refers to black and white, but it literally means a mixture.
8. Caterpillars.
9. Feral pigeon
10. Blackbird.

PUZZLE 8 – Fitword

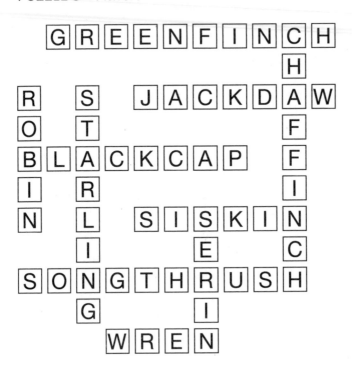

PUZZLE 9 – General Knowledge *What's Unusual?*

1. The male builds multiple structures (up to ten) known as 'cock-nests' to impress visiting females.
2. It's incredibly loud.
3. The female is much heavier (almost half as much again) than the male – in most birds, males are larger and heavier.
4. The sexes are alike, while in house sparrow they are very different.
5. It spends much of its time looking for and hiding acorns for its winter food stores.
6. It imitates.
7. It uses mud to plaster its nest hole to just the right specifications.
8. They will all be different colours or patterns. Other pigeons look similar to each other.
9. They will sometimes nest in artificial sites and man-made objects, like old jugs, kettles and teapots.
10. It consists almost entirely of ants.

PUZZLE 10 – Missing Words

1. It was the weekend of the RSPB's BIG Garden Birdwatch. I sat down in my kitchen to watch the comings and goings on the feeders.
2. What I needed to do was to observe my space for a whole HOUR and count the maximum number of each bird that I saw.
3. I am lucky that I have plenty of HOUSE sparrows, and these were the first birds that I saw.
4. This morning, there were plenty of gulls FLYING OVER but I couldn't count these, because birds only qualify if they land.
5. While I was watching the feeders, a predatory SPARROWHAWK made a rush at the feeders, hoping for a snack, but all the tits and finches got away.
6. One of the annoying things with this survey is that many bird rascals came along YESTERDAY and gorged themselves, but haven't turned up today.
7. It's not as if I don't put out enough food for them. I practically bankrupt myself buying Black SUNFLOWER or SAFFLOWER seeds.
8. And I'm very careful with bird hygiene. I always use 'no MESS' seed mixes so that less spills on the ground.
9. I was very excited to see some GREENFINCHES because they have suffered a great deal in this area from a horrible disease called Trichomonosis.
10. But in the end, the best bird of the day had nothing to do with the feeders. It was a grey WAGTAIL trotting around at the edge of the pond.

PUZZLE 11 – General Knowledge *Tits*

1. Blue tit
2. Crested tit
3. Marsh tit and willow tit
4. Long-tailed tit and bearded tit
5. Great tit
6. Simply put, they have extremely strong legs.

7. 1000
8. Great tit
9. Coal tit
10. Blue tit

PUZZLE 12 – Crossword

PUZZLE 13 – Multiple Choice *Garden Bird Voices*

1. a. Magpie
2. d. Great tit
3. a. Chaffinch
4. b. Song thrush
5. c. Collared dove

6. d. Starling
7. c. Carrion crow
8. a. Robin
9. b. House sparrow
10. d. House martin

PUZZLE 14 – Word Ladder

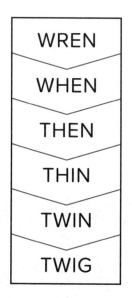

CROW
CROP
COOP
COOT
LOOT
LOST

WREN
WHEN
THEN
THIN
TWIN
TWIG

PUZZLE 15 – General Knowledge *Sleeping Arrangements*

1. Swift
2. Tawny owl
3. Blackbird
4. Wren
5. Robin
6. Long-tailed tit
7. Pigeons
8. Starling
9. Pied wagtail
10. Gulls, such as herring or black-headed

PUZZLE 16 – True or False? *Robins*

1. TRUE
2. TRUE
3. FALSE – the American robin is more closely related to the blackbird.
4. TRUE
5. TRUE
6. FALSE – female robins sing in the autumn, a lot.
7. FALSE – they absolutely do; in fact, on the continent their migration has been closely studied.
8. TRUE
9. FALSE – the female does.
10. FALSE – it's three to five.

PUZZLE 17 – Word Circle

BLACKBIRD. The other birds are the LARK and the RAIL.

Other words to find include: acid, acrid, aid, ail, air, alb, arc, arid, ark, back, bad, bail, bald, balk, bar, barb, bard, bark, blab, black, bra, braid, bridal, cab, cad, car, card, clad, crab, dab, dark, dial, drab, lack, lad, laid, lair, lard, liar, lira, rabbi, rabid, rack and raid.

PUZZLE 18 – Mix and Match *Garden Birds and Their Nests*

WOODPIGEON

A platform of twigs in a shrub or tree, so poorly constructed you can see the eggs from below.

HOUSE MARTIN

A cup of mud attached to a vertical surface, often under the eaves of buildings.

GREAT TIT

A cup made mostly out of moss, lined with grass and often feathers, placed inside a hole, often a nest box.

LONG-TAILED TIT

A remarkable domed nest made from moss and cobwebs, with lichen on the outside and 800–2,000 feathers stuffed inside.

GOLDFINCH

A very neat cup, woven with grass and moss and lined with copious plant down, often thistledown, placed towards the end of a tree or shrub branch.

CARRION CROW

A large cup of twigs and earth, placed high up in the upper branches of a tree.

MAGPIE

A large, domed structure of twigs, placed in the branches of a tree, sometimes quite low down.

HOUSE SPARROW

Often a bit of a mess, an unruly dome of grass in a bush or stuffed into a nest box, sometimes also a house martin nest.

GREAT SPOTTED WOODPECKER

A chamber in a tree, excavated by the parents, with no lining except for some chippings.

MALLARD

A shallow depression on the ground, made from grass and lined with the female's breast feathers.

PUZZLE 19 – What Bird Am I?

Coal tit

PUZZLE 20 – Codeword

The bird found in the shaded squares is the NUTHATCH. The two birds in the grid are the SPARROWHAWK and TREECREEPER.

PUZZLE 21 – General Knowledge *Finches*

1. Siskin
2. Bullfinch
3. Brambling
4. Bullfinch
5. Chaffinch
6. Goldfinch

7. It doesn't have a black cap.
8. Greenfinch
9. The juveniles don't have the striking colour on the head.
10. Greenfinch – it may nest in it, roost in it and perch on top of it!

CHAPTER TWO

Bird Behaviour

PUZZLE 22 – Mix and Match *Looking for Love?*

HOUSE SPARROW

A 'badge' of black on the chin

COOT

The size of the white forehead

BLUE TIT

The ultraviolet on the crown

SWALLOW

The length and symmetry of the tail

WREN

Nest-building prowess

PHEASANT

The spurs on the legs

GREENFINCH

The intensity of yellow in the wings

COMMON TERN

An ability to catch and bring fish

BLACKCAP

The density of vegetation in the territory

SEDGE WARBLER

The repertoire in the song

PUZZLE 23 – Fitword

PUZZLE 24 – True or False? *Bird Sounds*

1. TRUE
2. FALSE – it sometimes sings on the ground, too.
3. TRUE
4. TRUE
5. FALSE – it's usually about 20 minutes.
6. TRUE
7. TRUE
8. TRUE
9. FALSE – it's seasonal and a biological imperative.
10. FALSE – it can do this any time in spring.

PUZZLE 25 – Word Circle

INCESSANT.

Other words to find include: aces, acts, ancients, anise, antes, antics, antis, ants, ascent, ascents, ass, assent, asset, canes, canines, canniest, cans, cants, case, casein, cases, cast, caste, castes, casts, cats, cents, cites, east, eats, enacts, ices, inanest, inns, ins, insane, insect, insects, inset, insets, instance, instances, its, nascent, nest, nests, nets, nicest, nines, nits, sac, sacs, saint, saints, sane, sanest, sans, sat, sate, sates, satin, satins, scan, scans, scant, scent, scents, sea, seas, seat, seats, sect, sects, senna, sent, set, sets, sic, siesta, sin, since, sine, sins, sis, sit, site, sites, sits, stain, stains, stance, stances, stein, steins, sties, tans, teas, tennis, tens, ties, tines and tins.

PUZZLE 26 – Who Am I? *Parenting*

1. Cuckoo
2. Woodpigeon
3. Swift
4. Mallard
5. Great tit or marsh tit
6. Puffin
7. Blackbird
8. Marsh harrier
9. Coot
10. Grey heron

PUZZLE 27 – Multiple Choice *Unusual Behaviour*

1. a. Shrike
2. b. Moorhen
3. c. Black grouse
4. d. It may bring worms to the surface
5. a. Ants
6. c. Water weed
7. d. The parents carry young chicks on their back
8. Trick question – all are true!
9. d. They use a mid-air food pass
10. a. It wades in the water and then grabs a fish at its feet

PUZZLE 28 – Mix and Match

PUFFIN	1		**MOORHEN**	6
COLLARED DOVE	2		**GOLDCREST**	7
COMMON GULL	3		**MARSH TIT**	8
DUNLIN	4		**BLUE TIT**	9
HEN HARRIER	5		**PHEASANT**	10+

PUZZLE 29 – Codeword

The shaded squares can be rearranged to spell JUVENILE. The two additionally clued words in the grid are COURTSHIP and DUCKLINGS.

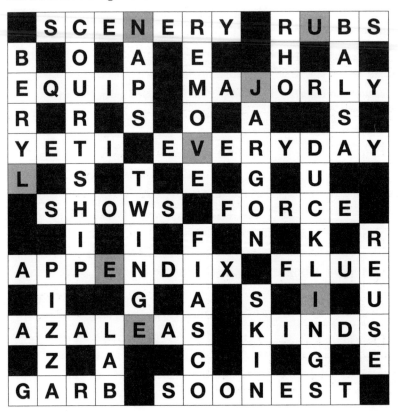

PUZZLE 30 – True or False? *Males and Females*

1. TRUE (!)
2. TRUE
3. FALSE – it's the female's choice, almost invariably.
4. TRUE
5. TRUE
6. TRUE – it happens mainly among seabirds, especially petrels.
7. FALSE – very few birds have a penis, although ducks do.
8. FALSE – no, that's largely the male's job.
9. TRUE
10. TRUE

PUZZLE 31 – General Knowledge *'Terms and Conditions'*

1. It's most often after the last egg is laid, although birds will sometimes do the first as well.
2. Turn the eggs over from time to time.
3. Brood
4. Nestling
5. Fledgling
6. Chick
7. Begging
8. Brooding
9. Cygnet
10. Juvenile

PUZZLE 32 – Pathfinder

1. WATER RAIL
2. SPOTTED CRAKE
3. GREAT TIT
4. MARSH WARBLER
5. NIGHTINGALE
6. CIRL BUNTING

The nightingale is particularly tricky to spot when skulking.

PUZZLE 33 – What Bird Am I?

Cuckoo

PUZZLE 34 – General Knowledge *Nests and Eggs*

1. An eyrie.

2. Generally pear-shaped, with one thinner end. This reduces its turning circle and, on the ground, ensures that it doesn't get lost. Also, four pear-shaped eggs fit neatly together.

3. They are usually white, or at least pale.

4. It only lays one egg, and the pattern is bold and unique – it may help the parents find the nest-site!

5. A heronry.

6. A rookery!

7. A colony of cormorants!

8. They sometimes lay extra eggs in next door's nest – it's known as egg dumping.

9. A small, sharp projection on the bill known as an egg-tooth.

10. Snails – their shells are made of calcium and help make egg shells.

PUZZLE 35 – Wordsearch *Bird Habits*

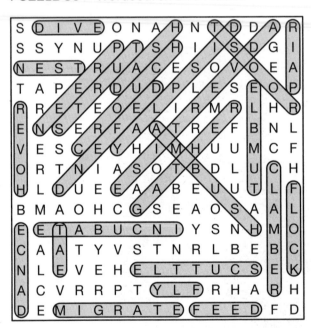

PUZZLE 36 – Multiple Choice *Bird Songs and Calls*

1. b. Goldfinch
2. d. Mute swan
3. b. Wren
4. a. Barn owl
5. d. Raven

6. c. Pheasant
7. b. Curlew
8. b. Wigeon
9. a. Crane
10. b. Swift

PUZZLE 37 – Mix and Match *Flocks*

KINGFISHER
Territorial

LAPWING
Territorial

AVOCET
Small colony

GOLDFINCH
Informal clumping of pairs

KITTIWAKE
Large colony

HOUSE MARTIN
Small colony

FIELDFARE
Informal clumping of pairs

HOUSE SPARROW
Small colony

BLACK-HEADED GULL
Large colony

ROBIN
Territorial

PUZZLE 38 – Crossword

PUZZLE 39 – Mix and Match

CHOUGH
Ants, beetles and other invertebrates

PTARMIGAN
Berries, seeds, shoots

DARTFORD WARBLER
Insects and spiders

CETTI'S WARBLER
Insects

WATER RAIL
Eats almost anything, even young birds

WHEATEAR
Insects and other invertebrates

GOSHAWK
Medium sized birds and mammals

DIPPER
Insects, especially their larvae

RED-THROATED DIVER
Fish

COMMON SNIPE
Worms and other invertebrates

PUZZLE 40 – Word Ladder

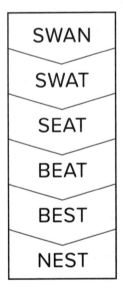

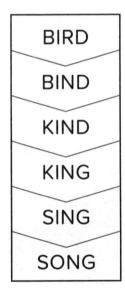

PUZZLE 41 – Multiple Choice *Displays and Courtship*

1. b. Great crested grebe
2. a. Red-breasted merganser
3. c. Greenfinch
4. d. Woodpigeon
5. a. Tree pipit

6. d. Whitethroat
7. b. Pheasant
8. c. Buzzard
9. d. Lapwing
10. b. Song thrush

PUZZLE 42 – True or False? *Self-care*

1. FALSE – it's from the Latin 'alus', meaning 'other'.
2. FALSE– the number of baths, if any, varies through the season and in different weather conditions.
3. TRUE – the sun's rays probably disperse parasites and may keep feathers supple.
4. TRUE
5. FALSE – it's ants, not flies.
6. FALSE
7. TRUE
8. TRUE
9. FALSE – sparrows and game birds bathe in dust and water, often on the same day.
10. TRUE

CHAPTER THREE

Coastal and Countryside Birds

PUZZLE 43 – Anagrams

1. House martin
2. Short-eared owl
3. Black guillemot
4. Common sandpiper
5. Garden warbler
6. Sandwich tern
7. Collared dove
8. Bearded tit
9. Lesser whitethroat
10. Stonechat

PUZZLE 44 – General Knowledge

1. Everything – it isn't a tit and it doesn't have a beard.
2. They steal much of their food from other birds, such as terns and auks.
3. The name 'marsh'.
4. Woodpeckers – this is how they withstand the impact of their pecking!
5. The kingfisher (the same species occurs there).
6. Yellowhammer
7. It floats
8. Merlin
9. Churring
10. Puffin

PUZZLE 45 – Pathfinder

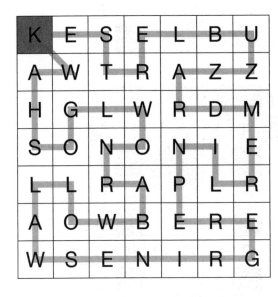

1. KESTREL
2. BUZZARD
3. MERLIN
4. PEREGRINE
5. SWALLOW
6. BARN OWL
7. GOSHAWK

The swallow is not a bird of prey.

PUZZLE 46 – True or False?

1. TRUE
2. FALSE – it can whistle and grunt. The name 'mute' comes from the fact it doesn't call in flight, using the sounds of its wings to keep in touch.
3. FALSE – Strictly speaking, scarecrows are designed to keep rooks away.
4. TRUE – some are 'hammerers' and some are 'stabbers'.
5. TRUE
6. FALSE – it's smaller than both.
7. FALSE – herring gulls 130,000 pairs; puffins 580,000 pairs.
8. TRUE
9. FALSE – they have a special adaptation – glands which filter the salt from the water; the salt is then excreted through their nostrils.
10. FALSE – each female is a specialist on only one species, whichever species reared it.

PUZZLE 47 – Codeword

The shaded squares can be rearranged to spell RAZORBILL. The four additionally clued words in the grid are BEACH, MARSH, RIVER and LAKES.

PUZZLE 48 – Odd One Out

1. Tufted duck is the only diving duck.

2. All have forked tails except for the long-tailed tit.

3. All are nocturnal except the turnstone.

4. All have been reintroduced in Britain except black guillemot.

5. All are recent arrivals as breeding birds in Britain, but only the collared dove found its way naturally.

6. They all nest in colonies in trees, except the Sandwich tern that nests on the ground.

7. Tricky this, but all have entirely black adult plumage except the blackbird, in which the female is brown.

8. They are all mainly green in colour except the green sandpiper (although half a mark for willow warbler, which doesn't have green in the name!)

9. They all nest in holes except the long-tailed tit.

10. They all regularly sing in flight except for the dunnock.

PUZZLE 49 – General Knowledge

1. Goldcrest (or firecrest)

2. Mute swan

3. Teal

4. Nightingale

5. The little owl!

6. Peregrine falcon – measurements vary, but it is generally agreed it can achieve at least 150 km/h (93 mph) in a vertical dive.

7. A 'V' shape. This helps conserve their energy, and birds take turns being at the front or back of the formation depending on their energy levels.

8. It retracts its neck. Storks and cranes hold their neck straight out.

9. They aren't ears – just tufts of feathers.

10. Bittern

PUZZLE 50 – Wordsearch *Waders*

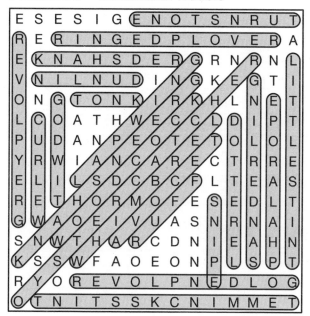

```
E  S  E  S  I  G  E  N  O  T  S  N  R  U  T
R  E  R  I  N  G  E  D  P  L  O  V  E  R  A
E  K  N  A  H  S  D  E  R  G  R  N  R  N  L
V  N  I  L  N  U  D  I  N  G  K  E  G  T  I
O  N  G  T  O  N  K  I  R  K  H  L  N  E  T
L  C  O  A  T  H  W  E  C  C  D  D  I  P  T
P  U  D  A  N  P  E  O  T  E  T  O  L  O  L
Y  R  W  I  A  N  C  A  R  E  C  T  R  R  E
E  L  I  L  S  D  C  B  C  F  L  T  E  A  S
R  E  T  H  O  R  M  O  F  E  S  E  D  L  T
G  W  A  O  E  I  V  U  A  S  N  R  N  A  I
S  N  W  T  H  A  R  C  D  N  I  E  A  H  N
K  S  S  W  F  A  O  E  O  N  P  U  S  P  T
R  Y  O  R  E  V  O  L  P  N  E  D  L  O  G
O  T  N  I  T  S  S  K  C  N  I  M  M  E  T
```

PUZZLE 51 – What Bird Am I?

1. Moorhen
2. Pheasant
3. Sanderling
4. Avocet
5. Kittiwake

6. Sand martin
7. Redwing
8. Stonechat
9. Eider
10. Cormorant

PUZZLE 52 – General Knowledge *Seabirds*

1. Hovering, followed by plunge-diving to catch fish.
2. Gannet
3. Many gulls regularly go inland.
4. They throw up a foul-smelling fluid.
5. Three
6. It is strongly pear-shaped. One of the theories is that this helps it to stay put on a cliff.
7. Orange-red, and it is pecked at by the chick to beg for food.
8. It jumps, even if hundreds of metres above the sea.
9. By smell.
10. To avoid being caught and eaten by predators, usually gulls or skuas, which are active by day.

PUZZLE 53 – Fitword

PUZZLE 54 – Multiple Choice

1. b. 76
2. d. 7,000
3. a. It shivers its tail
4. c. Heather shoots
5. d. Deciduous woods

6. c. 1996
7. d. Sessile oak woods
8. c. Wasp grubs
9. b. Eelgrass
10. a. Rocky coasts and jetties

PUZZLE 55 – Mix and Match

CETTI'S WARBLER
Reed beds and wetlands

CHOUGH
Coastal cliffs, crags

COMMON SNIPE
Wetlands and bogs

RED-THROATED DIVER
Small Scottish lochs and
sea coast

WHEATEAR
Rocky and stony places,
especially uplands

WATER RAIL
Marshes and reed beds

DARTFORD WARBLER
Lowland heathland

GOSHAWK
Large forests and nearby
open areas

PTARMIGAN
High, bleak mountain
plateaux

DIPPER
Fast-flowing streams

PUZZLE 56 – Crossword

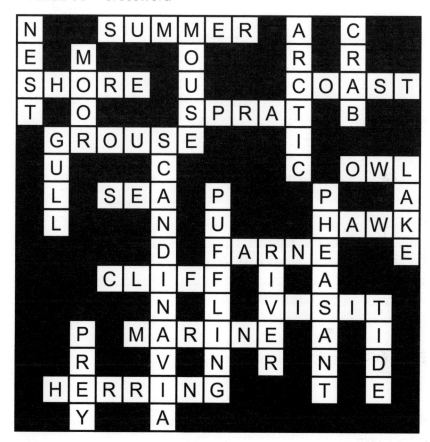

PUZZLE 57 – Mix and Match

CANADA GOOSE
White chin (as if it's cut itself shaving)

BLACK GROUSE
Lyre-shaped tail in male

STONE-CURLEW
Staring yellow eye

TURTLE DOVE
Black-and-white (zebra crossing) mark on neck

NIGHTJAR
Tiny bill conceals huge mouth

JAY
Kingfisher-blue patch on wing

SAND MARTIN
Brown band across chest

NUTHATCH
Black stripe through eye

SISKIN
Yellow wing-bars

BLACK GUILLEMOT
Bright red legs and feet

PUZZLE 58 – General Knowledge *Colours*

1. Pink
2. Chestnut (or similar)
3. Yellow
4. Yellow
5. Orange
6. Orange
7. Yellow
8. Blue
9. White – the colour could potentially reflect light into the cracks in tree trunks where the birds feed.
10. Black

PUZZLE 59 – Mix and Match *Special Places*

AVOCET
Havergate Island, Suffolk

WHITE-TAILED EAGLE
The Isle of Mull

CHOUGH
Lizard Point, Cornwall

CIRL BUNTING
Devon coast

OSPREY
Loch Garten, Highland

PUFFIN
Skomer Island, Wales

ARCTIC AND SANDWICH TERN
Farne Islands, Northumberland

STARLING (OR GREAT EGRET)
Somerset Levels

MANX SHEARWATER
Isle of Man

DARTFORD WARBLER
Dartford Heath, London

PUZZLE 60 – Word Ladder

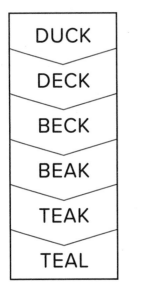

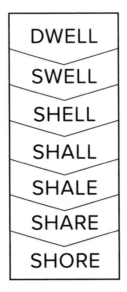

PUZZLE 61 – Multiple Choice *Waders (Shorebirds)*

1. a. Curlew
2. b. It nests in old nests above ground
3. d. Lek
4. a. It bobs up and down
5. a. Snettisham
6. b. Male and female reverse roles with male looking after eggs and young
7. c. Four
8. d. It is made by their tail feathers
9. a. Worms
10. b. It turns things over

PUZZLE 62 – Odd One Out *Bird Sightings*

1. c. Cirl bunting

   Cirl bunting only found on south coast of England.

2. d. Black grouse

   Black grouse extinct in Hampshire, red kite reintroduced.

3. c. Red kite

   Black grouse still in Hampshire, red kite extinct.

4. e. Long-tailed tit

   Long-tailed tit doesn't occur there.

5. c. Nightingale

   The nightingale has migrated away.

6. d. Collared dove

   Collared doves didn't appear in Britain until the mid-1950s.

7. c. Yellow grouse

   The yellow grouse doesn't exist.

8. e. Puffin

   Puffins should be out at sea.

9. a. Eastern bluebird

   Despite the song, a bluebird has never been recorded in Britain.

10. e. Wood warbler

    The wood warbler, as its name suggests, is a woodland bird.

PUZZLE 63 – Hidden Names

1. Sadly, things remain a LITTLE AUK-ward between us.
2. Get up. Don't just BEE-EATER-bout the bush.
3. She is gambling everything on this. She's a real high ROLLER.
4. It's three SHRIKES and you're out.
5. We're getting short of PETREL, we need to fill up.
6. It's important in life to know your LINNETS.
7. There are 24 HAWFINCHES making up a foot.
8. R-EGRETS, I've had a few.
9. It's been so cold that my fingers are frost BITTERN.
10. I will definitely accept that. I think you got it about TWITE.

PUZZLE 64 – Word Circle

GUILLEMOT.

Other words to find include: ell, elm, gel, gill, gilt, gimlet, glue, glum, glut, guile, guilt, gull, gullet, ill, leg, lei, let, lie, lieu, lilt, lime, lit, log, loge, lot, lout, lug, lute, melt, mil, mile, mill, millet, mogul, mole, motel, motile, moult, mule, mull, mullet, ogle, oil, tell, tile, till, toil, toll and tulle.

PUZZLE 65 – General Knowledge *Birds of Prey and Owls*

1. Osprey (also white-tailed eagle)
2. The meat of dead animals, technically known as carrion.
3. Sparrowhawk
4. Hobby
5. Buzzard
6. Kestrels tend to prefer mammals and sparrowhawks birds.
7. Hen harrier
8. Tawny owl – the 'tu-whit' call is quite separate from the 'tu-whoo' hooting and they aren't usually heard in sequence.
9. Barn owl – there is no bird called 'screech owl' in Britain.
10. Mountain hare.

CHAPTER FOUR

Bird Biology

PUZZLE 66 – Parts of a Bird

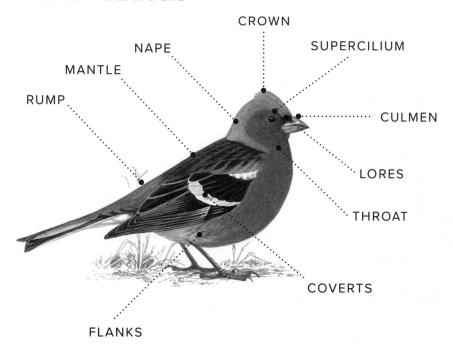

CROWN

NAPE

SUPERCILIUM

MANTLE

RUMP

CULMEN

LORES

THROAT

COVERTS

FLANKS

PUZZLE 67 – Word Circle

TAXONOMIST.

Other words to find include: ant, anti, antis, ants, atom, atoms, into, iota, iotas, its, mantis, mast, mat, matins, mats, mint, mints, mist, mitt, mitts, moat, moats, moist, moot, moots, most, motion, motions, motto, nit, nits, not, omit, omits, onto, ottoman, ottomans, saint, sat, satin, sit, snoot, soot, sot, stain, station, stint, stoat, taint, taints, tam, tams, tan, tans, tat, tax, taxi, taxis, tin, tins, tint, tints, tit, titan, titans, toast, tom, tomato, toms, ton, tons, too, toot, toots, tot, tots, toxin and toxins.

PUZZLE 68 – Mix and Match *Scientific Names*

MANX SHEARWATER
Puffinus puffinus

WREN
Troglodytes troglodytes

AVOCET
Recurvirostra avosetta

CETTI'S WARBLER
Cettia cetti

HOUSE SPARROW
Passer domesticus

HOBBY
Falco subbuteo

WATER RAIL
Rallus aquaticus

KNOT
Calidris canutus

TURTLE DOVE
Streptopelia turtur

MAGPIE
Pica pica

PUZZLE 69 – True or False?

1. FALSE – this is a common misconception although many can turn their heads up to 270 degrees in each direction.
2. TRUE – many species have different appearances between summer and winter.
3. TRUE – having hollow bones helps facilitate flight, and they are also present in flightless birds!
4. TRUE – one is for sleeping, one for blinking, and one for eye health.
5. FALSE – their nostrils are internal, opening in the mouth.
6. TRUE
7. FALSE – a swan may have eight times that of a hummingbird.
8. TRUE
9. FALSE – it's the other way round.
10. TRUE

PUZZLE 70 – Codeword

The shaded squares can be rearranged to spell CLASSIFY. The four additionally clued words in the grid are BEAK, FEET, HEAD and IRIS.

PUZZLE 71 – General Knowledge *Plumage*

1. Ptarmigan
2. Late summer
3. They can erect their body feathers to increase the amount of air between the skin and the outside and so lose less heat.
4. The rachis, or shaft
5. Barbs
6. Feather lice
7. White, blue and green
8. Iridescence
9. A short-lived cryptic plumage that birds acquire to cover for flightlessness or near-flightlessness.
10. Once grown, feathers are inert and wear out.

PUZZLE 72 – Multiple Choice *Senses*

1. b. One ear is higher up on the skull than the other.
2. c. × 2.2
3. c. Woodcock
4. a. Infrasounds
5. c. Through the eyes
6. b. Touch
7. d. Find specific plants for the nest.
8. b. Storm petrel
9. a. They can detect ultraviolet from the berries.
10. d. They do have taste buds that are on the tongue, bill tip and floor of the mouth.

PUZZLE 73 – Pathfinder

1. BARNACLE
2. CANADA
3. TAIGA BEAN
4. WHITE FRONTED
5. GREYLAG
6. PINK FOOTED
7. TUNDRA BEAN

The eighth goose is BRENT.

PUZZLE 74 – Finding Your Feet

a. Coot
b. Swift
c. Eagle
d. Sparrow
e. Duck
f. Heron
g. Grebe

PUZZLE 75 – True or False? *Fossil Birds*

1. TRUE
2. FALSE – many of the early birds had teeth.
3. FALSE – pterosaurs were an offshoot all their own, and weren't even closely related to dinosaurs.
4. TRUE
5. TRUE
6. FALSE
7. TRUE
8. FALSE – it's China.
9. TRUE
10. TRUE

PUZZLE 76 – Mix and Match *Families and Relatives*

SAND MARTIN
Swallow

GREY WAGTAIL
Meadow pipit

JAY
Jackdaw

GLOSSY IBIS
Spoonbill

EIDER
Mallard

REDPOLL
Bullfinch

RED KITE
White-tailed eagle

BLACKCAP
Dartford warbler

DUNLIN
Bar-tailed godwit

KESTREL
Merlin

PUZZLE 77 – Word Ladder

SORT
SORE
TORE
TYRE
TYPE

GENUS
MENUS
MINUS
MINES
MITES
CITES
CITED

PUZZLE 78 – General Knowledge *Bills*

1. Seed eating. These beaks are specialised for crushing seeds.
2. Eating invertebrates (bill used in probing).
3. Their food is ground up in a muscular stomach – the gizzard.
4. Ideal for probing in tight spaces.
5. Common snipe.
6. A female curlew has a longer, more curved bill than the male.
7. Nothing – the terms are interchangeable, although 'you cannot pay beaks'.
8. The female has orange on the lower mandible.
9. Their bills are serrated with fine 'teeth'. They are often called 'sawbills'.
10. Both upper and lower bill have an array of 'teeth' or lamellae, which overlap and make an efficient filter-feeding 'net'.

PUZZLE 79 – Multiple Choice *Flight*

1. a. Soaring
2. b. Gliding
3. d. Bearded tit
4. c. Hovering
5. d. 123 km/h (76 mph)
6. a. Quartering
7. a. V
8. c. Long, pointed wings
9. b. 166 km/h (103 mph)
10. c. Grey partridge

PUZZLE 80 – True or False?

1. TRUE – the rest can only scoop water up and then tilt it down the throat.
2. TRUE – this bone is where the flight muscles attach.
3. FALSE – it's all delivered in one go!
4. FALSE – it's a one-way system, not inhalation and exhalation of the same body of air.
5. TRUE
6. TRUE
7. TRUE
8. FALSE – they don't sweat.
9. TRUE
10. FALSE – it's the small intestine.

PUZZLE 81 – Crossword

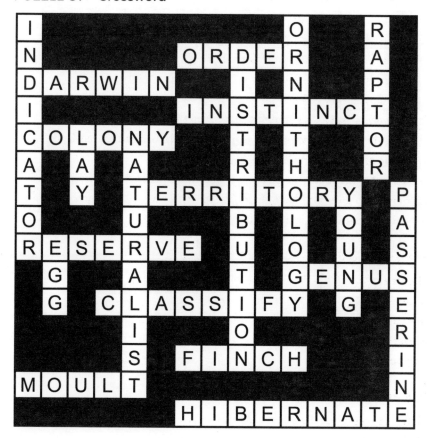

PUZZLE 82 – Hidden Names

1. Remarkably, ofFAL CONtinues to be eaten in the UK, mostly as black pudding.
2. Back in the 11th Century, King cNUT HATCHed a clever plan to show his humility to his English subjects by failing to hold back the tide.
3. Walking down by the riverside, I was delighted to see some flowering wateR AVENs (*Geum rivale*).
4. They all flew norTH, RUSHing to be the first on territory.
5. I hadn't realised that the party was over and was embarrassed to be the laST ONE CHATting.
6. The car's chasSIS KINd of buckled below us, which was disconcerting.
7. Look at the gorgeous detail on those beautiful, scarRED, POLLarded willows.
8. We enjoyed a long session looking up at the stars, despite the BITTER Night.
9. Both John StoneS AND ERLING Haaland are brilliant players for Manchester City.
10. Little George is enjoying his gift of DuPLO VERy much.

PUZZLE 83 – Wordsearch *Genus Species*

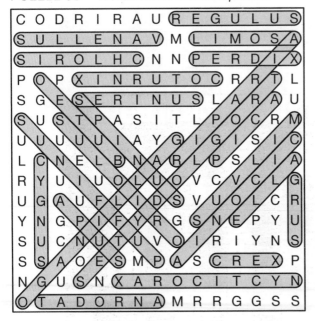

PUZZLE 84 – What Bird Am I?

Lapwing

PUZZLE 85 – Fitword

PUZZLE 86 – What Bird Am I?

Kingfisher

CHAPTER FIVE

A History of Birds

PUZZLE 87 – Crossword

PUZZLE 88 – Mix and Match *Breeding Pairs*

STARLING
1.6 million

WHITETHROAT
1.1 million

ARCTIC TERN
52,500

LITTLE EGRET
970

LESSER SPOTTED WOODPECKER 800

OSPREY
230

WIGEON
190

The first letters of each bird spell
SWALLOW – 625,000

PUZZLE 89 – General Knowledge *Introduced Species*

1. 17th century
2. Little owl
3. Golden Pheasant, Lady Amherst's Pheasant
4. Mandarin
5. Caucasus/Black Sea/Caspian region
6. White stork
7. Great bustard
8. Central Wales
9. Ruddy duck
10. France, Spain and Portugal (Iberia)

PUZZLE 90 – Multiple Choice

1. a. Wren
2. c. 71 per cent
3. b. Herring gull (130,000)
4. a. 1989
5. b. Turtle dove
6. c. 95 per cent
7. b. Cuckoo
8. a. Buzzard
9. d. Red List
10. d. Hen harrier

PUZZLE 91 – Wordsearch *In Decline*

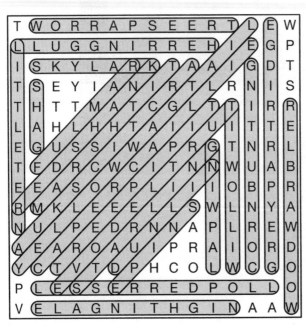

PUZZLE 92 – Codeword

The shaded squares can be rearranged to spell CURLEW. The two additionally clued words in the grid are ORNITHOLOGY and BIRDWATCHER.

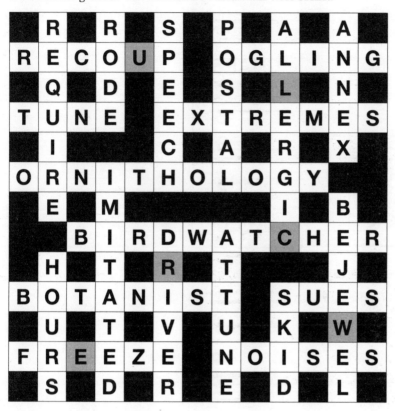

PUZZLE 93 – Pathfinder

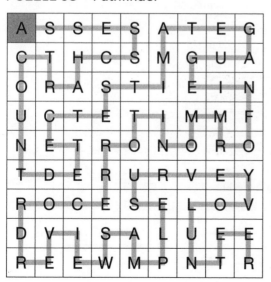

1. ASSESS
2. CHART
3. COUNT
4. DETECT
5. ESTIMATE
6. GAUGE
7. INFORM
8. MONITOR
9. RECORD
10. REVIEW
11. SAMPLE
12. SURVEY
13. VOLUNTEER

PUZZLE 94 – Word Ladder

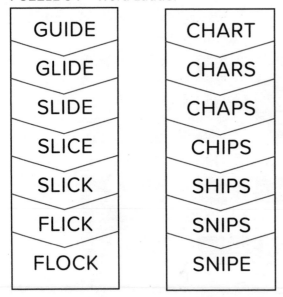

GUIDE	CHART
GLIDE	CHARS
SLIDE	CHAPS
SLICE	CHIPS
SLICK	SHIPS
FLICK	SNIPS
FLOCK	SNIPE

PUZZLE 95 – Mix and Match *Folk Names*

BLACK GUILLEMOT
Tystie

GARDEN WARBLER
Pettichaps

LONG-TAILED TIT
Bottle jug

RINGED PLOVER
Dulwilly

SONG THRUSH
Throstle

MISTLE THRUSH
Storm cock

GREAT SKUA
Bonxie

GOLDFINCH
Thistle warp

DUNLIN
Plover's page

AVOCET
Scooper

PUZZLE 96 – Word Circle

KITTIWAKE. The three other birds are KITE, TIT and TWITE.

Other words to find include: ate, eat, eta, kit, take, tat, tea, teak, teat, tie, tweak, wait, watt, wet and wit.

PUZZLE 97 – Multiple Choice *Dates*

1. a. 1638
2. a. 1416
3. b. 1889
4. c. c. 580
5. d. 1959

6. c. 1959
7. b. 1979
8. a. 1939
9. b. 2005
10. b. 1960

PUZZLE 98 – Fitword

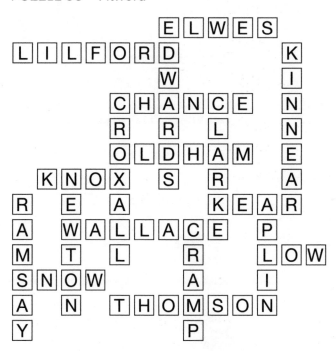

PUZZLE 99 – Mix and Match *Gains and Losses*

A	B	C
COLLARED DOVE	WRYNECK	DARTFORD WARBLER
GREAT EGRET	KENTISH PLOVER	GREY PARTRIDGE
CETTI'S WARBLER	RED-BACKED SHRIKE	CRESTED TIT

PUZZLE 100 – Mix and Match *Collective Nouns*

SKYLARK
An exaltation

STARLING
A murmuration

CARRION CROW
A murder

GOLDFINCH
A charm

SPARROWHAWK
A cast

ROOK
A parliament

RAVEN
An unkindness

SNIPE
A wisp

GREYLAG GOOSE
A skein

GREAT SPOTTED WOODPECKER
A descent

CHAPTER SIX

What's That Bird?

PUZZLE 101 – Mix and Match

1. WHINCHAT
2. COMMON BUZZARD
3. CORN BUNTING
4. BEE-EATER
5. WHITE STORK
6. SWALLOW
7. STARLING
8. TREE SPARROW

PUZZLE 102 – What Bird Am I? *Male or Female*

1. Eider
a. Female
b. Male

2. Cuckoo
a. Male
b. Female

3. Lesser spotted woodpecker
a. Female
b. Male

4. Teal
a. Male
b. Female

PUZZLE 103 – Spot the Difference *See pages 266–7*

PUZZLE 104 – What Bird Am I?

a. Waxwing
b. Lapwing
c. Great crested grebe
d. Rook
e. Grey partridge
f. Grey heron
g. Song thrush
h. Wigeon
i. Mallard
j. Jackdaw

PUZZLE 105 – Spot the Difference *See pages 268–9*

PUZZLE 106 – Mix and Match *Juveniles*

1. LITTLE OWL
2. PEREGRINE FALCON
3. CURLEW SANDPIPER
4. GOSHAWK
5. WOODPIGEON
6. SHELDUCK
7. PUFFIN
8. TAWNY OWL

PUZZLE 107 – What Bird Am I?

1. Blue tit
2. Goldcrest
3. Hawfinch
4. Marsh tit

5. Green woodpecker
6. Song thrush
7. Raven
8. Great spotted woodpecker

PUZZLE 108 – Mix and Match

1. MARSH WARBLER
2. MISTLE THRUSH
3. BLACKCAP

4. BLUETHROAT
5. SKYLARK
They are all songbirds

PUZZLE 109 – What Bird Am I?

1. Blackbird
2. Grey wagtail
3. Nuthatch
4. Magpie

5. Crossbill
6. Goldfinch
7. Jay
8. Crested tit

PUZZLE 110 – Spot the Difference *See pages 270–1*

PUZZLE 111 – What Bird Am I?

1. Bullfinch
2. Wren
3. Kingfisher
4. Great tit

5. Robin
6. Capercaillie
7. Yellowhammer
8. Greenfinch
9. Collared dove

CHAPTER SEVEN

Birds In Culture

PUZZLE 112 – Missing Words *Phrases and Expressions*

1. Lark
2. Goose
3. Crow
4. Duck
5. Swallow
6. Swan
7. Chicken(s)
8. Peacock
9. Albatross
10. Coot

PUZZLE 113 – Fill in the Gap *Movie Titles*

1. Cuckoo's
2. Falcon
3. Eagles
4. Geese
5. Swan
6. Mockingbird
7. Pelican
8. Hawk
9. Kite
10. Sparrow

PUZZLE 114 – General Knowledge *Culture, Legends and Folk Tales*

1. Storks
2. Raven
3. Wisdom
4. Magpie
5. Gulls
6. Sparrows
7. Swans
8. Magpies – but it isn't true at all!
9. It's completely false!
10. In plain sight – they just look very like the adults. In common with many birds, young pigeons stay in the nest until fully grown in size.

PUZZLE 115 – General Knowledge *Culture*

1. *The Lark Ascending*
2. Blackbird
3. Owls
4. The Housemartins
5. Bill Oddie
6. Nightingale
7. 24 (four and twenty)
8. Cuckoo
9. William Shakespeare. Back in the 16th and 17th centuries red kites would have been a familiar sight, associated with death and decay.
10. Gilbert White

PUZZLE 116 – Mix and Match *Football Teams*

THE SEAGULLS
Brighton and Hove Albion

THE CANARIES
Norwich City

THE OWLS
Sheffield Wednesday

THE MAGPIES
Newcastle United, Notts County

THE ROBINS
Bristol City, Charlton Athletic,
Cheltenham Town, Swindon Town

THE EAGLES
Crystal Palace

THE BLUEBIRDS
Cardiff City

THE SWANS
Swansea City

PUZZLE 117 – Missing Words *Famous People*

1. Swann
2. Partridge
3. Jay
4. Crow
5. Parrott
6. Hawke
7. Swift
8. Martin
9. Wren
10. Nightingale

PUZZLE 118 – General Knowledge *Christmas*

1. It's a ground bird.
2. North America.
3. Mute, whooper and Bewick's.
4. Black ('coaly') – they may have been blackbirds.
5. The shortest day (21 or 22 December).
6. Tropical Africa.
7. Postmen (they were all men in those days) were called 'Robins' after their red uniforms.
8. Quite apart from cold, the snow obscures their feeding places.
9. They are almost extinct in Britain.
10. Robin.

CHAPTER EIGHT

A Rare Sight

PUZZLE 119 – Word Ladder

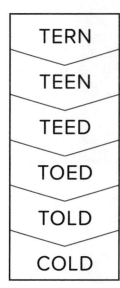

TERN
TEEN
TEED
TOED
TOLD
COLD

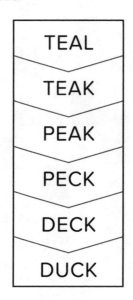

TEAL
TEAK
PEAK
PECK
DECK
DUCK

PUZZLE 120 – What Bird Am I?

Alpine swift

PUZZLE 121 – General Knowledge

1. Great auk
2. Great auk
3. A lammergeier
4. Collared dove
5. Against all the odds, a male and female met up and bred in Scotland.
6. Black-browed albatross
7. It was best seen from a Tesco's car park!
8. They all breed in Europe but have never been recorded in Britain.
9. Balearic shearwater
10. They were once extremely rare but are now recorded much more frequently.

PUZZLE 122 – Codeword

The shaded squares can be rearranged to spell RED LIST. The two additionally clued words in the grid are HAWFINCH and NIGHTJAR, both on the Red List.

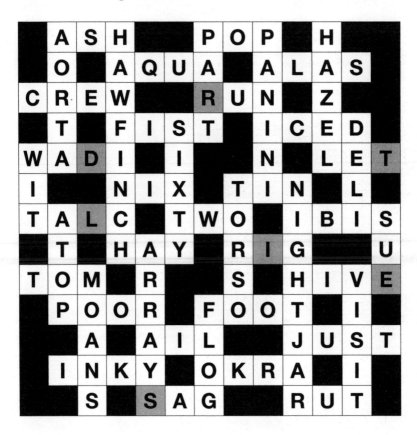

PUZZLE 123 – Mix and Match *Where Do They Come From?*

PALLAS'S SANDGROUSE
Central Asia

WHITE-CROWNED BLACK WHEATEAR
North Africa

WALLCREEPER
Mountains of Europe

PURPLE SWAMPHEN
Southern Europe

ALLEN'S GALLINULE
Tropical Africa

AQUATIC WARBLER
Eastern Europe

MAGNIFICENT FRIGATEBIRD
Caribbean

IVORY GULL
Arctic Ocean

NORTHERN MOCKINGBIRD
USA

SIBERIAN BLUE ROBIN
Far Eastern Asia

PUZZLE 124 – True or False?

1. TRUE
2. FALSE
3. TRUE
4. TRUE
5. TRUE
6. FALSE – it doesn't immerse at all.
7. TRUE
8. FALSE – it was DNA of the droppings!
9. FALSE – it's another host of the common cuckoo.
10. TRUE

PUZZLE 125 – Wordsearch *Hard to See*

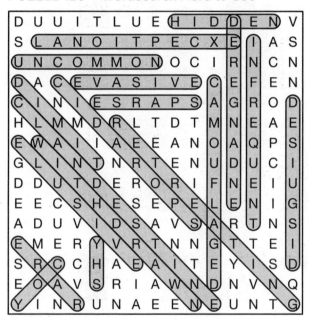

PUZZLE 126 – General Knowledge *Stunners*

1. Berries
2. Supermarket car parks – they are often planted with berry-bearing shrubs.
3. It batters the insect to death.
4. Yellow and black.
5. It 'rolls' in flight display.
6. They often impale dead prey on thorns (or barbed wire) as a temporary food store.
7. Wallcreeper
8. It raises its crest.
9. Its advertising call is 'hoo-poo-poo'.
10. Ortolan bunting

PUZZLE 127 – Odd One Out

1. c. Bee-eater (in lowlands, not mountains).
2. d. Pallas's warbler (not from the USA).
3. c. Ross's gull (the only one without at least one largely white plumage).
4. d. Black-winged curlew (doesn't exist).
5. d. Red-rumped swallow (the others hardly ever land).
6. a. Blue-winged teal (feeds on surface, doesn't normally dive).
7. d. Roller (others hover).
8. b. Fan-tailed warbler (Zitting Cisticola) (others have long tails).
9. b. Western olivaceous warbler (not a conifer specialist).
10. a. Short-toed eagle (eats snakes, others eat insects).

PUZZLE 128 – Mix and Match *Whose Bird?*

GULL
James Clark Ross

OWL
Peter Gustaf Tengmalm

PETREL
Robert Swinhoe

EIDER
Georg Wilhelm Steller

WARBLER
Paolo Savi

SANDPIPER
Spencer Fullerton Baird

SANDGROUSE
Peter Simon Pallas

SWAN
Thomas Bewick

BUNTING
Philipp Jakob Cretzschmar

GUILLEMOT
Morten Thrane Brünnich

PUZZLE 129 – Crossword

PUZZLE 130 – Anagrams

1. Alpine swift
2. Siberian thrush
3. Brown booby
4. American wigeon
5. Mourning dove

6. Desert wheatear
7. Penduline tit
8. Alpine accentor
9. Squacco heron
10. Long-tailed skua

PUZZLE 131 – Missing Words *Place Names*

1. Egyptian nightjar or Egyptian vulture (Egyptian goose)
2. Tennessee warbler
3. Dalmatian pelican
4. Spanish sparrow
5. Baltimore oriole

6. Baikal teal
7. Caspian gull, Caspian plover, Caspian tern
8. Alpine swift, alpine accentor
9. Iberian chiffchaff
10. Ascension frigatebird

PUZZLE 132 – Fitword

```
K           G L O S S Y   D
E                   W       U
N   C   S U R F     I B I S
T   A   C           F       K
I   S T O N E C H A T       Y
S   P   T           L
S H R I K E         P
C   A   R O S E F I N C H
A   N       I       N
U   G       B A L E A R I C
P       G   U   E   R
  W A R B L E R   S   C
      E   L   I   S   T
      A       A M E R I C A N
O R T O L A N   R   C
```

PUZZLE 133 – What Bird Am I?

1. Rose-coloured starling
2. Pallas's sandgrouse
3. Ivory gull
4. Black-winged stilt

5. Eleonora's falcon
6. Red-backed shrike
7. Spoonbill
8. Short-toed treecreeper

PUZZLE 134 – Multiple Choice *Seabirds*

1. b. Frigatebird
2. c. Wilson's petrel
3. a. Sooty tern
4. d. Double-crested cormorant
5. b. It was seen on a boating lake far inland.
6. a. It was taken back to the Caribbean but died before release.
7. d. It was misidentified as another species of frigatebird for 50 years.
8. b. Red-billed tropicbird
9. b. Black-browed albatross
10. c. It couldn't be assigned a species, so isn't officially on the British List. Although definitely a giant petrel, there are two almost identical species, and it couldn't be assigned to either.

PUZZLE 135 – Word Circle

BLACK KITE. The small, dabbling duck is the TEAL.

Other words to find include: abet, able, ace, act, ail, albeit, ale, alike, ate, back, bail, bait, bake, bale, balk, bat, batik, beak, beat, beta, black, bleak, bleat, cab, cable, cake, cat, cleat, eat, eta, kale, lab, lace, lack, lake, late, lea, leak, tab, table, tack, tackle, tail, take, talc, tale, talk, tea and teak.

PUZZLE 136 – General Knowledge *Across the Pond*

1. Brown-headed cowbird
2. Wandering tattler (*Tatler*)
3. Northern mockingbird
4. Snow goose
5. American robin
6. Indigo bunting
7. Purple martin
8. Yellow-bellied sapsucker
9. Wood thrush (or hermit thrush)
10. Eskimo curlew

PUZZLE 137 – Half Anagrams

Gulls	**Sandpipers**	**Warblers**
1. Bonaparte's	4. Least	7. Icterine
2. Sabine's	5. Semipalmated	8. Lanceolated
3. Slaty-backed	6. Pectoral	9. Magnolia
		10. Cape may

PUZZLE 138 – Pathfinder

G	R	E	N	G	R	E	I	S	H	W	A
W	N	E	O	C	L	E	N	C	R	E	R
I	A	L	L	E	A	F	T	I	••	L	B
N	E	T	S	S	E	D	R	N	G	T	A
G	E	D	E	O	T	••	I	I	Y	N	W
L	E	Y	R	O	F	E	N	L	P	I	T
L	G	S	W	E	D	W	A	R	I	P	
O	E	I	H	R	R	A	T	E	R	U	O
W	L	T	I	P	E	G	S	D	C	O	L
U	R	E	P	I	A	T	O	S	E	I	P
M	D	S	D	L	I	V	R	T	I	P	D
P	E	A	N	O	L	E	B	A	C	K	E

1. GREEN-WINGED TEAL
2. LESSER YELLOWLEGS
3. WHITE-RUMPED SANDPIPER
4. RED-FOOTED FALCON
5. GREENISH WARBLER

6. CITRINE WAGTAIL
7. OLIVE-BACKED PIPIT
8. ROSE-COLOURED STARLING
9. TAWNY PIPIT

PUZZLE 139 – What Bird Am I? *So Near . . .*

1. Greater flamingo
2. Black woodpecker
3. Alpine chough
4. Pygmy cormorant

5. (White-winged) snowfinch
6. White-headed duck
7. Black-shouldered kite
8. Lesser spotted eagle

CHAPTER NINE

Avian Migration

PUZZLE 140 – Mix and Match *Month by Month*

JANUARY

The RSPB's Big Garden Birdwatch is held.

FEBRUARY

Traditionally, this is the month when the highest numbers of wild ducks are counted in Britain.

MARCH

The first sand martins arrive in Britain.

APRIL

The first cuckoo is heard calling in Britain.

MAY

International Dawn Chorus Day is celebrated.

JUNE

Broods of tits are disgorged in vast quantities from the production lines that are their nests.

JULY

This is probably the main month of moulting for most of the birds of Britain.

AUGUST

The last swifts normally depart from Britain.

SEPTEMBER

Robins start singing again after their summer break.

OCTOBER

The first redwings, fieldfares and wild geese begin to arrive in force to spend the winter in the UK.

NOVEMBER

Song thrushes usually begin to sing their territorial songs.

DECEMBER

Masses of starlings are gathering in their communal roosts at the end of the year's shortest days.

PUZZLE 141 – Fitword

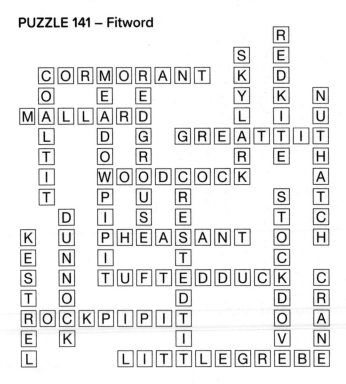

PUZZLE 142 – General Knowledge

1. Arctic terns. They have a round trip of 35,000 km (21,750 miles) each year; some of them go to Antarctica or even circumnavigate the Antarctic continent.

2. It sees more daylight each year than any other animal.

3. Bar-tailed godwit. It can go over 11,000 km (6,835 miles), although this is the Alaskan population travelling to New Zealand.

4. Staging areas

5. Fat

6. Return journeys – individuals are in a hurry to get to a territory before their rivals.

7. Using the stars or moon to orientate.
   Not overheating.
   Usually more gentle meteorological conditions.
   Using sunset as guide.

8. It normally flies throughout the whole journey and winter without touching down at all.

9. A fall (or fallout).

10. The sea – or more precisely, sea crossings, because they prefer to use thermals, which don't form over water.

PUZZLE 143 – Wordsearch

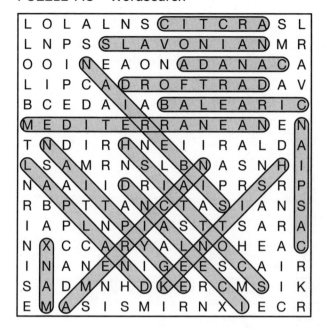

PUZZLE 144 – Mix and Match

1. **GOLDFINCH**
   Central and southern France

2. **BLACKCAP**
   Southern Spain

3. **KITTIWAKE**
   Central Atlantic Ocean, between
   UK and USA

4. **RING OUZEL**
   North Africa

5. **WILLOW WARBLER**
   West Africa (Sahel region)

6. **LESSER WHITETHROAT**
   East Africa

7. **COMMON TERN**
   Waters off West Africa

8. **SWALLOW**
   Cape Province, South Africa

9. **MANX SHEARWATER**
   Off the coast of southern
   South America

10. **ARCTIC TERN**
    Antarctica

PUZZLE 145 – Multiple Choice *Migration*

1. c. Leapfrog migration
2. b. Differential migration
3. a. Crane
4. d. Water pipit
5. a. It is when different individuals from the same regional population either migrate or stay put.

6. c. Loop migration
7. b. Garganey
8. a. Dartford warbler
9. d. Swallow
10. d. Spotted flycatcher

PUZZLE 146 – Codeword

The shaded squares can be rearranged to spell KINGFISHER. The two additionally clued birds in the grid are FIRECREST and CORMORANT.

PUZZLE 147 – Mix and Match *Tracked Migration Routes*

1. **OSPREY**
2. **TURTLE DOVE**
3. **SWIFT**
4. **NIGHTJAR**
5. **CUCKOO**

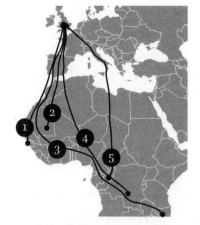

PUZZLE 148 – True or False? *Finding the Way*

1. TRUE

2. FALSE – most birds have their migration programmed into them individually, inheriting it from their parents.

3. FALSE – they have an internal clock that compensates for the sun's movement.

4. TRUE

5. TRUE

6. FALSE – they learn the movement of constellations around the poles.

7. TRUE – the further you are towards a pole, the greater the angle of incidence of the magnetic field.

8. TRUE

9. FALSE (probably)

10. TRUE (probably!)

PUZZLE 149 – Mix and Match *Song Calendar*

The perfect mix and match is as follows, 2 points each.

JANUARY – Dipper

FEBRUARY – Blackbird

MARCH – Chiffchaff

JUNE – Reed warbler

JULY – Yellowhammer

AUGUST – Woodpigeon

SEPTEMBER – Wren

OCTOBER – Tawny owl

NOVEMBER – Mistle thrush

DECEMBER – Great tit

Otherwise, 1 point each.

DIPPER – October, November, December

BLACKBIRD – March, June, July

CHIFFCHAFF – June, July

REED WARBLER – July

YELLOWHAMMER – March, August

WOODPIGEON – Almost any month

WREN – Almost any month

TAWNY OWL – November, January, February, March

MISTLE THRUSH – December, January, February, March

GREAT TIT – January, February, March

PUZZLE 150 – Word Ladder

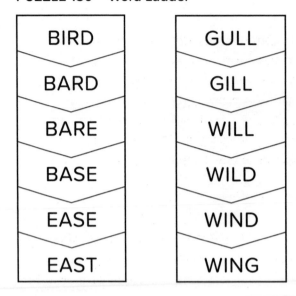

BIRD	GULL
BARD	GILL
BARE	WILL
BASE	WILD
EASE	WIND
EAST	WING

PUZZLE 151 – What Bird Am I? *Personal Timekeeping*

1. Swift
2. Sand martin
3. Pink-footed goose
4. Redwing/fieldfare
5. Cuckoo

PUZZLE 152 – General Knowledge *Berried Treasure*

1. Mast
2. March and April (range January–May)
3. February to April – wild autumn seeds run out and insects only increase slowly.
4. They are white.
5. Caterpillars
6. Goldfinch
7. Flying ants
8. Earthworms
9. Insects (especially caterpillars), then seeds.
10. The adults can use the bloom of fledgling birds nearby to catch for their own young.

PUZZLE 153 – Word Circle

PTARMIGAN.

Other words to find include: again, agar, aim, air, airman, amp, ant, anti, apart, aping, apt, aria, arm, arming, armpit, art, atria, gain, gait, gap, giant, gnat, grain, gram, grant, impart, inapt, main, man, mania, map, mar, margin, marina, mart, mat, mating, migrant, nag, nap, pagan, pain, paint, pair, pan, pang, pant, par, paring, part, parting, pat, patina, pita, pram, prating, rag, raga, rain, ram, ramp, rampant, ran, rang, rant, rap, rapt, rat, rating, tag, taming, tan, tang, tap, taping, tapir, tar, tiara, train, tram, tramp, tramping and trap.

PUZZLE 154 – Multiple Choice *Weather*

1. d. Hail
2. b. Swift
3. a. The sun could overheat eggs or chicks.
4. d. Frost
5. c. Ice
6. b. 10m/s
7. c. The only insects available are close to the ground.
8. d. Worms are harder to reach in the baked ground surface.
9. c. Too wet
10. a. Anticyclone

PUZZLE 155 – Crossword

PUZZLE 156 – True or False?

1. TRUE – it can manage nearly 1,000 km (621 miles) in 24 hours, which will be more than many non-migrants will ever fly.
2. FALSE – they normally fly below 1,500 m (4,920 ft).
3. FALSE – in autumn, huge numbers of birds arrive to spend winter here, such as thrushes, geese, gulls and finches.
4. TRUE – some seabirds swim at least part of the way, and a few birds around the world (game birds, emus) walk.
5. FALSE – birds often make mistakes and are well able to correct them.
6. FALSE – many birds make short flights of a few tens of kilometres, especially at the beginning of their journeys.
7. FALSE – some birds, such as redwings and fieldfares, make completely different migratory journeys from one year to the next, and many birds change journeys according to circumstances.
8. FALSE – birds often move around in winter.
9. TRUE
10. FALSE – most birds can't see particularly well in the dark.

PUZZLE 157 – Missing Words *Dangers*

1. Fat
2. Wrong direction
3. Rain, snow or hail (all correct)
4. Sea
5. Light
6. Wind
7. Fog
8. Bird of prey
9. Shot
10. Desert
11. Stop

PUZZLE 158 – Multiple Choice *Warblers*

1. b. Dartford warbler
2. a. Willow warbler
3. b. Wood warbler
4. c. Chiffchaff
5. a. Sedge warbler
6. d. Marsh warbler
7. c. Blackcap
8. c. Common whitethroat
9. a. Yellow-browed warbler
10. d. Garden warbler

PUZZLE 159 – Pathfinder

Q	U	A	I	N	C	H	A
A	E	I	H	T	H	G	T
T	E	L	W	I	N	I	N
E	E	B	W	O	G	A	L
R	C	O	R	L	L	A	E
A	R	C	N	R	E	W	S
K	S	P	Y	T	E	P	I
E	O	R	E	☆	T	I	P

1. QUAIL
2. WHINCHAT
3. NIGHTINGALE
4. SWALLOW
5. BEE-EATER
6. CORNCRAKE
7. OSPREY
8. TREE PIPIT

PUZZLE 160 – What Bird Am I? *Migrant*

Swallow

PUZZLE 161 – What Bird Am I? *Personal Timekeeping*

1. Chiffchaff
2. Blackcap
3. Puffin
4. Shelduck
5. Manx shearwater

PUZZLE 103 – Spot the Difference

PUZZLE 105 – Spot the Difference

PUZZLE 110 – Spot the Difference

ACKNOWLEDGEMENTS

I wish to thank Nicky Crane, my commissioning editor, for all her hard work in keeping this project together, and for all her encouragement and good sense. Also, I wish to thank Trevor Davies at Octopus for thinking of me.

Big thanks too to my wife, Carolyn, whose help with this book was essential, and whose enthusiasm with quizzes in general was so infectious that it now feels as though she wrote it!

Dominic Couzens

Huge thanks to my colleague Laura Jayne Ayres for her help in preparing the codewords, crosswords, fit words, pathfinders, word circles, word ladders and wordsearch puzzles in this book. And of course an equally big thanks to all at Octopus for the privilege of being able to work with Dominic and the RSPB on this book.

Dr Gareth Moore

PICTURE CREDITS